FOR
EARTH'S
SAKE

STEPHEN BEDE SCHARPER

FOR
EARTH'S
SAKE

Toward a Compassionate Ecology

Edited and with an Introduction
by Simon Appolloni

Foreword by Dr. James Orbinski

NOVALIS

© 2013 Novalis Publishing Inc.

Cover design: Angel Guerra
Layout: Audrey Wells
Interior images: iStockphotos; ooyoo (p. 25), Megan Lorenz (p. 59), Ken Canning (p. 125)

Published by Novalis

Publishing Office
10 Lower Spadina Avenue, Suite 400
Toronto, Ontario, Canada
M5V 2Z2

Head Office
4475 Frontenac Street
Montréal, Québec, Canada
H2H 2S2

www.novalis.ca

Library and Archives Canada Cataloguing in Publication

Scharper, Stephen B.
    For earth's sake : toward a compassionate ecology / Stephen
Bede Scharper; edited and with an introduction by Simon
Appolloni ; foreword by James Orbinski.

Includes bibliographical references.
ISBN 978-2-89646-521-7

    1. Environmental ethics. 2. Human ecology.
I. Appolloni, Simon, 1962- II. Title.

GE42.S33 2012   179'.1   C2012-904119-X

Printed in Canada.

We acknowledge the financial support of the Government of Canada through the Canada Book Fund for business development activities.

6 5 4 3 2   17 16 15 14 13

I wish to thank my wife, Katie Newton, and daughter, Elena Appolloni, for their help on the journey, and my father, Lucio Appolloni and siblings, Luisa, Suzanne, and Andrew Appolloni, and sister-in-law, Janine Appolloni, for their encouragement and enthusiasm. I would also like to thank Nancy Lunney, Steven Waring, Hilary Cunningham, and Jocelyn Kealey for their care and inspiration. Most importantly, I wish to thank Stephen Scharper for trusting me with a good portion of his life's work.

— *Simon Appolloni*

I first wish to thank Simon Appolloni for his careful gathering and framing of my writings—all performed with humour and professional aplomb. I am also indebted to Libby Stephens, my first editor at the *Toronto Star*, for her editorial guidance (and acerbic wit), as well as Ian Urquhart, Andrew Phillips, Fred Edwards, and John Cruickshank, all of whom have been consistently supportive of and patient with my meanderings through their editorial pages.

In addition, Joseph Sinasac and Grace Deutsch of Novalis have been a delight to work with, as has Anne Louise Mahoney, whose gentle editorial wisdom has enriched both this volume and the author.

Finally, to my wife, Hilary, whose brilliant mind and winsome grace infuse all my writings—and my spirit—thank you.

— *Stephen Bede Scharper*

To my students,
past and present,
for enlivening me
with their dreams and visions.

Stephen Scharper

Table of Contents

Foreword

As humans, we need a new way of seeing, and from it a new way of being. Not only are we the proverbial frog in the cooking pot, but we are also turning up the heat. While *all* is nature—even we humans—it is only humans that are changing the nature of nature. June 2012 was the hottest month ever recorded (since 1880). Globally, drought, flooding, fire, and all manner of adverse weather events abound. Even the most stalwart of conservative thinking recognizes that something is seriously wrong. The July 2, 2012, editorial of *The Financial Times* drily noted that "simply letting climate change rip and tidying up the damage as it occurs is not an enviable strategy."[1]

The environmental crisis demands a major re-examination of the underpinnings of the Western—and soon to be planetary—culture of globalization. Indeed, we are today in the midst of converging global crises in food, fuel, climate, economy, and governance. Each of these crises have both local and global causes, are interdependent, and, as we know all too clearly, have highly contagious global consequences. We are at a moment in our human story where we must squarely face the unavoidable complexity, interdependency, and fragility of our human and ecological condition. We have become our own geological epoch, the *Anthropocene*, where human pressures on the planet are at risk of triggering abrupt and irreversible changes with potentially catastrophic outcomes for human societies and for other life forms. We have already crossed three of nine planetary boundaries—or tipping points—and risk triggering non-linear, abrupt environmental change within continental and planetary biospheric systems.[2] As crises converge and ramify in unexpected ways, policy spheres can no longer be distinct. Global warming is not merely a matter of policy domains and frameworks. It is also a matter of justice. The *Financial Times* editorial went on to comment that "in poor countries, higher temperatures will mean an increased risk of hardship and societal collapse, and rich countries will be forced to respond."

The microbiologist Louis Pasteur said some 150 years ago that "the microbe is nothing, its terrain everything."[3] The implications of our global ecological and human context are staggering, to say the least. As Stephen Scharper notes in this wonderful book, "our current ecological moment is so grave … that it compels us to rethink the basic question of what it means to be human" (p. 66).

Scharper is right, too, when he says, "They are ultimately, no matter how we colour and contour them, spiritual and religious questions" (p. 67). And they are questions that our old and current ways of seeing cannot answer. We need a new story. Nature does not tell stories; we do. We find ourselves in them, choose ourselves in them, make ourselves in them. And if we are the stories we tell ourselves, we had better choose them well.

Scharper's book offers a carefully crafted selection of his twenty years of reflection on ecology, social justice, and spirituality. For me, one line set me adrift into a realization that a new way of seeing—a new story—is possible. Scharper recalls eco-theologian Thomas Berry, who once quipped that maybe it's time to "put the Bible on the shelf for twenty years and listen to nature" (p. 54). In reading these words, I instantly recalled my always repeatable sense of Awe when I paddle my canoe, with one of my children paddling in the bow, through the lake mist of pre-dawn; when I see life teeming around me in cycles of night and day in the wet mist between sky and water—cycles of beginnings and endings and beginnings again. In such moments there is a sense—just a sense, but an overwhelming sense—of all that has been before me, and will be long after me. And with each stroke of the paddle, I feel the life, and feel the actions in me, and through my children, too. I see the actions that sustain life, make life, give life—

actions that are but one form of the myriad forms of love. It is an Awe that is knowable, but overpoweringly self-evident when I simply feel it through me, around me. And it is an Awe that both humbles and empowers in a swell of beauty and seduction.

Perhaps it is that beauty and seduction is nature's tool for survival, because in some very real ways, we both become and protect what we fall in love with. And as I recalled this—as I felt it—as if from the same place, my mind instantly carried me to my experiences of the self-evident and overpowering compassion and outrage of humanitarian action that responds to human suffering and injustice. I remembered that same feeling of both humility and empowerment. Both moments fill me with Awe, and from it with action that draws me into the next action, and the next. And from beauty and seduction come hope and the inevitability of possibility.

A character in the British comedy movie *The Best Exotic Marigold Hotel*[4] says with an Indian sideways head nod, "India is great, because in the end, everything always works out. If things haven't worked out, it's not yet the end!" Martin Luther King said that "Any cultural movement will fail if it can't paint a picture of a world where people want to go to." We won't fail. Too many of us know Awe. But we need a new story, one rooted in an ethical framework that honours dignity and our interdependence, that pursues equity, and that is humble about our place in, and impact on, our beautiful home called Earth.

In this book, Scharper has crafted an opening, an invitation to a New Story, a new way of seeing and being. It is an invitation to Awe, to humility, to beauty and seduction; an invitation to fall in love, for earth's sake, and for our own.

James Orbinski OC, MSC, MD, MA

Dr. Orbinski is Research Chair and Professor in Global Health, Dalla Lana School of Public Health; Co-Director, Global Health Diplomacy Program, Munk School of Global Affairs; and former President of the International Council of Médecins sans frontières (Doctors Without Borders) at the time the organization received the 1999 Nobel Peace Prize.

Introduction

Our Current Context

It's really, really hard to escape it. We hear gloomy environmental news from experts almost daily: "Scientists say…" "The US government estimates…" "According to the United Nations…" and "Environmental disaster feared as worst in decades…."

Take water, for instance. By 2025, we are told, fresh water will be very scarce throughout most of the globe, severely affecting over a quarter of the world's human population and countless other species. If future scarcity isn't enough of a concern, even now millions of people, most of them children, die every year from diseases associated with inadequate water supply, sanitation, and hygiene. Glaciers and land-based ice sheets are melting owing to the warming of the climate, which contributes to rising sea levels, threatening disaster to low-lying areas around the globe. And oil spills, pollution from land, overfishing, and the warming of waters brought on by climate change are not only causing vast extinctions of fish and other sea life, but are altering a whole interconnected global ocean system, the main vehicle of life on Earth.

It's not just water. Almost a quarter of the world's mammals face extinction within 30 years. An area of rainforest the size of Austria is deforested each year. Rainforests are where most of the world's plant and animal species live; in one area of 25 acres of rainforest in Borneo, for example, about 700 species of trees were identified; to get an idea how big a deal that is, consider that in all of North America, there are no more than 700 tree species in total.

And it's not just "over there," either, is it?

Closer to home, scientists are finding a chemical soup in North American lakes, rivers, and streams, containing everything from antibiotics, natural and synthetic hormones, blood lipid regulators, anti-depressants, anti-inflammatories, painkillers, tranquilizers, chemotherapy drugs, drugs used to treat epilepsy and lower blood cholesterol, disinfectants, and a family of chemicals called phthalates, found in many cosmetics, perfumes, and hair products. If current trends with urban sprawl continue, by 2031 sprawl will cover an additional 1070 square kilometres of wetlands, forest, and farmland in the Greater Toronto Area alone. Already in the United States, in the past two centuries, one third of farmland topsoil has been blown or washed away. And speaking of farms, in Kansas, where farmers have been exposed to herbicides for 20 or more days a year, they are six times more likely to develop non-Hodgkin's lymphoma than are non-farmers. The prevalence of this disease is linked to the herbicide 2,4-D. Indeed, today the average person's body contains 250 chemicals that did not exist 50 years ago.

Whoa! Breathe...

If you are like me, hearing all this news about environmental and social devastation – day in and day out – generates a whole range of emotions: from angry, sad and worried to scared. Even if we somehow manage to hide ourselves from newspapers, magazines, TV and Internet news, YouTube videos, or tweets, who among us hasn't seen our favourite park, forest, or creek disappear to development, becoming the parking lot for a Mega-Stuff-Mart of some sort?

I remember as a kid playing almost all day and every day in the summer in a ravine just a stone's throw from my home in Toronto. It was a wild and fantastic place full of marshes, frogs, creepy crawlies of all kinds, and rambunctious kids with lots of imagination. I'll never forget the day I found a beetle the size of my fist. I couldn't keep my eyes or hands off it. To use today's lingo, it wasn't an "ew!" moment; it was an "OMG!" experience. That ravine is still there, but it is so manicured and "cleaned up" that the wildest thing you see now are two dogs on leashes stopping to sniff each other.

Angry, sad, worried, scared … aren't these emotions we feel when we lose something dear to us? And the real kicker is that we have only ourselves as a species to blame. Whether because of the growth of megacities, the effects of a large human population, or the chemical and biological effects of human activity, including greenhouse gases, there isn't a place on the planet, not even the South or North Poles, where human activities have not made their mark.

Our actions have been changing the Earth on a scale comparable with some of the major events of the ancient past. Most of us have heard of geological time units such as Jurassic – that period of time some 200 million years ago when there were flying reptiles and dinosaurs. Geologists call our relatively short period of time the Holocene, a time after the last Ice Ages and the initiation of the modern warmer and drier climate. However, the Geological Society of London – an association of scientists responsible for naming Geological Time Units – is considering naming our present time the *Anthropocene*, which is a formal way of saying that it is *human activity*, especially since the Industrial Revolution 300 years ago, that has been responsible for significantly altering the Earth.

Keep breathing: deep breaths, in, out…

These global realities stir deep emotions within us; I know they do in me. In many cases, we are probably unaware of the feelings they produce in us. But there is nothing wrong or shameful in recognizing that we feel pain – after all, never before has a species been responsible for bringing about the end of a geological era. While these realities arouse emotions in us, they can also lead to confusion and uncertainty: confusion about the root of our problem, and uncertainty about where to turn or what to do.

This book can help. For over 20 years, Stephen Bede Scharper has taught and worked as an editor, professor, and "civic scholar," seeking and forging connections among issues of spirituality, ecology, and social justice. In reflecting upon on the faith and fate of the Earth, he concludes that our current context confronts us with very sobering questions, questions of a deeply philosophical and spiritual nature that touch on not only ecology, but a global economic system that has consigned over one billion persons to absolute poverty:

- What is our role here?

- What is the vocation of the human as species?

- What kind of world do we wish to leave to future generations?

- What is the goal of "civilization" if its thrust forward leaves behind the world's ecosystems and a vast swath of the animal species as veritable roadkill?

- What *on Earth* are we doing?

Sobering questions indeed. The readings in this book – collected from the writings of Scharper, from a range of publications – have been chosen and arranged in a manner to help readers respond to each one of these questions, and to face our current realities with inspiration to turn things around. But Scharper is not proposing any ready-made, just-add-water solution to our woes. No, it's far more involved than that. Indeed, it's *how* Scharper suggests we respond to these questions that makes this book unique.

Falling in Love

Picture this: a classroom – more like an auditorium; it seats 500, and the University of Toronto's Introduction to the Environment class is full. After discussing some of the more overwhelming details of the devastation brought upon our planet by the work of human hands, Scharper asks his students, "Now, how does it make you feel?"

Feel?

This may seem like an odd question for a professor to ask, especially considering it's being asked in a public and prestigious university. But then again, Scharper is not your typical university professor. He is utterly serious when he explores the emotional dimensions underpinning our global environmental crisis. He maintains, "We can make ourselves more knowledgeable, change all our laws, fashion new policies, and even design cutting-edge sustainable technologies, but none of these will take hold until we change our relationship with the planet and indeed the universe." In short, Scharper invites us to fall in love.

Love?

In a way, yes. He suggests, in the language of environmental pioneer Aldo Leopold, that we need to develop a "love, respect, and admiration" for the biotic community of which we must begin to see ourselves as being "just plain members and citizens." He expands this relational approach toward the biotic "other" to include the universe itself. We are not just part of a biotic community on Earth, then: we are citizens of the entire universe!

What soon becomes clear in reading this book – or in taking his class – is that our search for a new ethic for our time is really a spiritual quest. For a new ethic to evolve, we must enter into a deeper communion not only with the planet, but also with the cosmos. In doing so, we develop a profound sense of the beauty of the natural world and are drawn to admire it. We come to see ourselves as "human self-reflecting agents amid a variety of non-human subjects," as Scharper says in "From Community to Communion." The natural world we love, respect, and admire becomes, in the words of Scharper's mentor, Thomas Berry (1914–2009), a communion of subjects rather than a collection of objects to be bought, sold, used, and discarded.

But a new ethic cannot develop solely with the recognition of ourselves as being "just plain citizens" of the larger natural community. Scharper reminds us that we cannot overlook the fact that the majority of human beings in the world are not even granted the status of citizen, let alone "plain citizen." Ignored by market and consumerist interests of the affluent, or forsaken by cost-benefit analyses of technocrats, the vast majority of the human species does not have access to the basic necessities of life, such as clean water, food, shelter, and education. They are further denied the right to self-determination, to define their own future and participate effectively in decisions affecting their lives.

What does all this have to do with an ethic for the biotic community, you ask?

Scharper shows how the processes that deny intrinsic value to plants and animals while conferring special status on some humans more than others are the same processes that downgrade the poor to "non-person" status. Of the vast majority of humans who are poor today, many live in the global South (sometimes referred to as the "Third World," or "developing world." ("Developing world," as readers will find out in Scharper's article entitled "Option for the Poor," is an inappropriate term; anyone who has been fortunate enough to travel, work, or live in such places knows that the people, their societies, and their cultures, although certainly lacking access to many basic human rights, are in many ways more "developed" than our Western so-called developed societies. As Scharper puts it, "These societies in the global South are already developed. The problem is that they are also exploited.") However, a notable number of humans, we must remember, also eke out a living among the wealthy in the global North. The poor, Scharper avers, are "often excluded environmentally," by which he means they are "literally displaced" to make way for, in some cases, mega projects like hydro-electric dams, or well-intentioned ecological projects that displace local communities. These humans bear an uneven burden of the devastation of the natural world in what Scharper describes as "unequal ecologies."

Put another way, we cannot think of the environmental degradation that surrounds us, and the oppression or exclusion of poor persons – who represent the majority of the human population today – as separate and distinct realities. The rejection of the status of "citizenship" to humans *and* the natural world are interrelated: both, Scharper maintains, are inextricably intertwined in a structure of "sin."

All this means that when we talk about an environmental ethic, we must locate the entire world human population squarely in the centre of deliberations on environmental issues. There is no environment "out there" apart from the human. We *are part of* the environment. And while we might be just plain citizens of the environment, we cannot escape the fact that we presently sit in the truck driver's seat of its destruction, while deflecting the resultant burdens we cause onto already marginalized populations, who are demoted to cargo-status in the trailer.

A New Ethic – Making Space for a Novel and Possibly Enhanced Way of Life

We begin to see why positioning the human and our role in the world becomes vital to Scharper. The questions he asks above are key. We have to examine ourselves, our role in the world, and how we are affecting future generations before we can adequately address the present global environmental crisis and growing economic disparity. The reason why we are in this mess, in large part, lies in inadequate, and in some cases fatally flawed, understandings of the human being.

In this book, Scharper calls for a shift away from an anthropo-centric ethic to an anthropo-harmonic ethic. The last chapter of this book explains in detail what he means by this term. A good way to understand the ethic is as a reinvention of the human as "just plain citizen" living in harmony with a larger biotic and cosmic community. It's an ethic designed to keep pace with our power as a species. Think of it this way: we have codes and penalties to deal with our power to destroy ourselves (suicide), to destroy another human (homicide), and even to destroy entire cultures (genocide). But we have no codes to deal with our power to destroy entire ecosystems (biocide) or our planet (geocide).

As we saw above, we cannot deal with such deep concerns properly until we change our relationship with the planet and, indeed, the universe, which brings us to the most important part of Scharper's anthropo-harmonic ethic: falling in love.

Like any relationship of love, this will involve fundamental changes in the form of sacrifices. Now, some of you might want to put the book down and walk away at this point. After all, who wants to hear about sacrifice? But stay with us. The last section of this book contains a short article entitled "On Sacrifice, Spirituality and Silver Linings." In this article, Scharper recounts the time he and his wife decided to give up their car. At first, his wife saw this as an Earth-shattering suggestion.

After all, the car is almost like a human appendage to many of us these days. It ranks just under food and housing as a fundamental requirement for survival. But notice what happened as the story unfolds. The whole family began registering unforeseen benefits, both spiritual and material: their lives became richer with less consumption, less stress, and they experienced greater family bonding. He concludes: "It's not just about sacrifice, but about making a space for a novel and possibly enhanced way of life. It may also hold hidden harvests for the spiritual and material well-being, not only of our families and nation, but of our larger household, the Earth."

The Design and Approach of the Book

Scharper's system to address our ecological crisis and deepening poverty is fundamentally Christian and liberationist in its foundation, with its concept of a "suffering God" who feels and shares the pain of creation. While broadly characterized as political theology, an easier way to think of his approach is the exploring of one's faith from the viewpoint of the oppressed, alienated, and suffering of our world – and not just humans, either. It is a down-to-Earth way of looking at our world, at creation, in a way that is self-critical and open to myriad other insights, models, and ways of knowing the world.

The book is designed so readers can participate in Scharper's analysis and reflections.

It is divided into three sections:

- Section I: Revealing—The Pain of Loss and the Delight in Wonder

- Section II: Reflecting—What on Earth Are We Doing?

- Section III: Redeeming—A Creative Space for New Life-giving Relationships

Each of the three sections begins with a short introduction to its theme and content; terms and concepts are explained. At the end of each section, readers will find questions that invite further reflection, along with exercises constructed to help us fall in love with creation. Readers can ponder these questions on their own or as a group.

Each section includes short articles originally written by Scharper for the *Toronto Star,* Canada's largest daily newspaper; an interview with him; and longer essays that have also been published elsewhere. (Because the pieces are from a range of sources, spelling and style vary slightly.) Publication dates for the articles are found in "Sources," towards the end of the book. The shorter articles are intentionally interspersed throughout each section to emphasize certain themes or to draw readers' attention to complementary issues. The concluding chapter is an original work that is set up in the form of an interview I conducted with Scharper. It teases out the salient features of his anthropo-harmonic ethic, while tying all his work together.

Finally, an appendix outlines suggested readings and documentaries you might wish to consult for more information on the subjects touched upon in this book: many of the books and some videos Scharper refers to in his articles can be found here.

In a sense, the book's structure is designed to mirror Stephen Scharper's teaching approach and his attitude to public scholarship, as it invites readers to participate deeply with mind, body, and heart in examining the fate and faith of Earth from critical and preferential vantage points. Should readers of this book ever be fortunate enough to find themselves in one of his classes or seminars, they will embark on a similar "whole-person reflective journey," perhaps hearing or even learning bird calls; taking field trips to a small natural forest sanctuary on campus; observing a meditation room, complete with a "living wall," at the university's Multi-Faith Centre for Spiritual Study and Practice; visiting the only sustainably designed Catholic church in Canada; directly engaging scientists, indigenous activists, and politicians in meaningful dialogue; or listening to Scharper recite passages and poetry from ecological literature while in a creative exchange with a professional violist in the background, as she improvises sounds and melodies off Scharper's cadence and tone. It's an effective—albeit uncommon—process for university pedagogy. But as I said earlier, Stephen Bede Scharper is not your typical university professor.

Simon Appolloni

SECTION I

Revealing—The Pain of Loss and the Delight in Wonder

Introduction

I felt a generational tether had been severed,
and grieved the fact the waters and woods that helped shape us
in our youth were no longer there to help frame and contour
the lives of our sons.

Stephen Bede Scharper

As the title suggests, this first section reveals what we have been doing to the planet and to one another, and the pain of loss we feel because of our actions. It also presents us with a summary of a wide variety of spiritual, social scientific, and cosmological approaches that many thoughtful thinkers, Christian ethicists, and social scientists of our time have taken to try to address our problems.

You will notice how Scharper's writings capture a way of seeing that relates two or more occurrences that have hitherto been assumed to be unconnected in society: for example, environmental degradation *and* economic disparity; feelings of loss *and* the awesome delight of a sunset. He does this to reveal patterns that invite us to caution, while simultaneously sparking awareness in us that fights indifference.

The notion of "anthropocentrism" is introduced in this section. This term comes from the Greek word *anthropos,* which refers to the "human." Coupled with "centric," the term denotes a tendency for human beings to regard themselves as the central and most significant entities in the universe or, as I like to put it, an "it's-all-about-us attitude." Not all people use the word in the same way, though, as you will see throughout this book. Some, like cultural historian Lynn White Jr., who is mentioned in "The Ecological Crisis: Moment Two," embraces the meaning mentioned above. Others, such as some ecofeminists and liberation theologians, employ the term with much less emphasis on the human—an "anthropocentrism-light," if you will.

This description helps us understand other terms used in this book: from the same Greek root *anthropos*, we also get the term "anthropogenic." "Genic," from the Greek *genesis*, refers to "origin," "creation," or "generation." Hence, "anthropogenic" refers to humans as the cause of something. As an example, for the anthropocene discussed in "Green Dreams: Religious Cosmologies and Environmental Commitments," you will often hear people labelling it "anthropogenic." Similarly, Scharper's anthropo-harmonic ethic, which is mentioned in the introduction to this book and fleshed out later on, describes the human living in harmony with the rest of creation. The full meaning and implications of the anthropo-harmonic ethic will be made clear in the conclusion.

Finally, in "The Ecological Crisis," Scharper puts forth some disturbing facts about our historical-socio-ecological moment, which feed into our pain of loss. At the time he originally wrote this paper (1998), this data was certainly correct. Almost a decade and a half later, most of the facts are still accurate, with the exception of two disturbing developments: while we did indeed surpass the 6 billion mark for human population, as Scharper forecasted, as you read this book today, the human population has already surpassed the *7 billion* mark. As for the information Scharper mentions about 1998 representing "the hottest year on record," we now know that 1998 is the only year *from the 20ᵗʰ century* that represents one of the top 10 warmest years on record (with records beginning in 1880). Moreover, the reader should note that according to James E. Hansen, the Director of NASA's Goddard Institute for Space Studies, the first 11 years of the 21ˢᵗ century experienced notably higher temperatures compared to the middle and late 20th century. Therefore, as of 2012, as stated on NASA's website, the year 2011 represents the ninth-warmest year on record.

What do these gloomy facts—some of which have gotten alarmingly worse—tell us? As greenhouse gas emissions and atmospheric carbon dioxide levels continue to rise, scientists expect the long-term temperature increase to continue. This tells us that these lamentable records for "warmest year on record" will most likely continue to be broken as well.

Simon Appolloni

Reverend Billy's Crusade against the "Shopocolypse"

"As fall turns to winter, many millions will converge on centres of worship large and small to celebrate and give thanks to a familiar god. He tells us to buy now and pay later. He tempts us with promises of endless credit as he leads us down the path to eternal debt..."

So begins *What Would Jesus Buy?* a just-in-time-for-the-holidays documentary that, at times mockingly, at times movingly, excoriates the "religion of consumerism," decries Mickey Mouse as the "Antichrist," and warns of the imminent "shopocalypse," whereby all persons, things, and values will be rendered mere commodities.

Think of it as a type of comedic, anti-consumerist, cinematic Christmas card, and you begin to get the vibe of this outlandish yet unexpectedly poignant film.

The energetic paladin of this message is anti-globalization activist Billy Talen, who, as Reverend Billy, replete with shock of bleached blond hair and evangelical preacher histrionics, traverses the United States with his wife and choirmaster Savita D., the Stop Shopping Choir, and the Not Buying It Band to proclaim the gospel of non-consumption.

An amalgam of Michael Moore, Bruce Springsteen, Jimmy Swaggart, and Borat, Reverend Billy prowls the parking lots of shopping malls and dances down church aisles exhorting Americans to repent of their mindlessly consumerist ways, "confess" their "shopping sins" (Rev. Billy actually sets up a confessional box), and wake up to a faith that doesn't come from a mall.

Interspersed throughout the odyssey are interviews with psychologists, anti-sweatshop activists, and real preachers, such as Jim Wallis, founder of the Sojourners community in Washington D.C., who buttresses Billy's message with facts and faith-based reflections on the hijacking of Christmas as a "drive-buy" culture.

As it turns out, many of the facts the film unveils are less than merry. For example, for the first time since the Great Depression, U.S. household personal savings are below zero, and 60 percent of American consumers are venturing out to the malls this December with at least $13,000 worth of long-term debt on high-interest credit cards. In addition, this Christmas, folks south of the border will spend half-a-trillion dollars and create 5 million tonnes of extra waste. A ho-ho no-no.

Add to that the fact that people in the U.S.—reputedly the most Christian nation in the world—now spend fewer than one hour a week in spiritual activities compared with more than five hours a week shopping, and that 15 million Americans may be clinically addicted to shopping, and you get a sense of the spiritual and psychological trappings of Billy's crusade.

The film's producer, Morgan Spurlock, producer of the 2004 documentary *Supersize Me*, said Talen "uses humour to make us laugh and make us look at really important things," adding that "if you can make somebody laugh, you can make somebody listen."

Rev. Billy, with his white suit and collar and red-robed choir, invades Minnesota's Mall of America, the main cathedral of U.S. consumerism.

The mall boasts its own police force, an amusement park, a wedding chapel, six kilometres of storefront, and National American University, the first university campus built inside a shopping centre. It hosts more than 42 million visitors per year, which, according to the film, exceeds the annual visitor tally to Washington D.C., Mount Rushmore, the Grand Canyon, and Disneyland combined.

As is his wont, Billy gets up close and personal with the mall police as they escort him from the premises.

With the final words of Rev. Billy, speaking of Christmas as the celebration of a child who would grow up and teach peace, the film touchingly shifts from the satirical to the spiritual.

Rev. Billy, like the heart-enhanced Grinch, realizes that Christmas does not come from a store, and that "Christmas, perhaps, is a little bit more."

It's ironic that it takes an ersatz preacher to remind a so-called Christian culture of this message.

The Rise of Nature Deficit Disorder

In speaking with a friend recently, I experienced a profound sense of loss. He had taken his son fishing, returning to the ponds and streams we fished together in our youth.

"Steve," my friend said, "they're all gone—Warner's Pond, Caddy's Pond—they're both filled in, and the North Woods is just one big housing development."

I felt a generational tether had been severed, and grieved the fact the waters and woods that helped shape us in our youth were no longer there to help frame and contour the lives of our sons.

This sense of "nature loss" also disturbs U.S. journalist Richard Louv, whose recent book, *Last Child in the Woods: Saving Our Children from Nature Deficit Disorder*, probes environmental, social, psychological, and even spiritual implications of the removal of nature from our children's lives. Reflecting on his childhood in the 1950s, Louv recalls that while no one then spoke of acid rain or the thinning ozone layer, he and other kids did have an intimate knowledge of the woods and fields near their homes. "A kid today," he writes, "can likely tell you about the Amazon rainforest—but not about the last time he or she explored the woods in solitude, or lay in a field listening to the wind and watching clouds move."

Louv cites several factors for the decline, including development of rural spaces, parental safety concerns, and liability restrictions on unsupervised play.

Claiming that North American society teaches youth "to avoid direct experience with nature," he writes that this lesson is taught by schools, families, even outdoor education groups, and is codified into community legal statutes. "Our institutions, urban/suburban design, and cultural attitudes unconsciously associate nature with doom— while dissociating the outdoors from joy and solitude."

In the "patent-or-perish" environment of higher education, he continues, we witness "the death of natural history as the more hands-on disciplines, such as zoology, give way to more theoretical and remunerative microbiology and genetic engineering."

And the post-modern notion that all reality is only a social construct, Louv writes, suggests "limitless human possibilities; but as the young spend less and less of their lives in natural surroundings, their senses narrow, physiologically and psychologically, and this reduces the richness of human experience."

Louv's work builds on the research of Harvard biologist E.O. Wilson, whose idea of "biophilia" suggests that humans have a natural love of and affinity for nature, and when access to the natural is blocked, these become distorted.

Louv also cites numerous psychological studies indicating the importance of nature exposure in helping children overcome attention deficit disorder and other medical and psychological challenges.

Interestingly, such research also jibes with the insights of Catholic priest and "geologian" Thomas Berry, who speaks of the "soul-loss" experienced each time a meadow or forest is developed into a shopping mall or parking lot.

Louv's work is not all nostalgic lament. Reflecting on land restoration movements, increased awareness around climate change, and scientific research about the importance of exposing children to nature, he hopes not only his sons, but all generations, may experience a rebirth of wonder in nature.

Green Dreams: Religious Cosmologies and Environmental Commitments

Imagine, for a moment, that you are living in the early 1800s in the settlement of York on the shores of Lake Ontario near present-day Toronto. Day and night, you hear a distinctive sound like ocean waves breaking—an undulating, unrelenting roar. Yet it is the sound not of water but of wind blowing through the old-growth forest of maple, beech, white pine, and oak that spreads west to present-day Windsor and beyond to Michigan, north to the Cambrian shield and east to the Ottawa Valley and the St. Lawrence. Early European settlers noted this sound in their journals, and some found it deeply unsettling.

In fewer than 200 years, 95 percent of that forest has been cut down. We shall not be haunted by that forest wind again in our lifetime, nor will our descendants be for many lifetimes to come.

Now think of a place in nature that was special to you growing up. Perhaps it was at a cottage, a field, pond, lake, woods, even a park or backyard in a city, a place where you could go to think, to wonder, to collect your thoughts and yourself.

Think about that place today. Does it still exist? Has it been filled in? Paved over for housing or condos, perhaps a Walmart or mall or a McDonald's? If so, how did this "development" make you feel? Did it engender a sense of loss? Did you chalk it up to the inexorable march of progress, or did you see it as a "body blow" to your spirit? If you did experience it as a spiritual loss, you have a small taste of what some First Nations perhaps felt when their sacred lands were removed from them and "developed."

As Marina Herrera, a Native American cultural critic and religious educator, avers,

> Harmony with creation is grounded deeply in one's relationship with the land. For most Native Americans, it is impossible to speak of a personal identity apart from the land. The earth grounds us not only geographically but also psychologically. As my grandmother told me, when I lost touch with Mother Earth, I misbehaved. When I attended to the land, however, my behaviour improved. In other words, the land itself can heal ... The land becomes the means for transcending time and reaching through to other generations.[1]

We are, as a human community, facing what many see as a "global environmental crisis." According to the plurality of the world's atmospheric scientists, we are, through fossil fuel emissions and other noisome activities, altering the climate of the planet and forcing perhaps thousands of species into extinction each year. Although the sources of the dinosaur extinction some 65 million years ago remain highly contested (Gary Larson of *The Far Side* has his own theory—smoking), the sources of the present species loss are all too clear—human pollution and destruction of habitat, most conspicuously that of tropical rainforests. We are destroying these cornucopias of life and oxygen at the rate of one football field per second, an area the size of Austria, each year. When we include other numbing ecological horrors—acid rain, overpopulation, poisoned air, ozone depletion, toxic waste sites, water contamination, poverty, militarization—we see environmental studies rivaling economics for the sobriquet "the gloomy science."[2]

Were the human race to receive a report card from the Creator for its stewardship of the Earth at the dawn of the third millennium, it would likely read, "Does not play well with other species."

Religions around the world are re-examining both their precepts and practice in light of ecological concerns. It is almost as if there has been a power failure, and the religious traditions are scouring their respective attics for candles from their heritage—a St. Francis of Assisi here, the Hebrew notion of Sabbath for the Land there, a Buddhist conception of *ahimsa*, or "non-harm," an Islamic notion of the human as "vicegerent" of creation—anything that may help illuminate a new path through our current ecological darkness.

Sundry faith traditions are also linking environmental and social justice issues in cogent ways. The UN State of the World Reports over the past decade indicate an alarming statistic—40,000 children younger than 5 die daily owing to environmental pollution, particularly tinctured water. From Walkerton, Ontario, to Cairo, Egypt, thousands of children are dying before their time owing to the twin funereal cairns of poverty and pollution. Religions around the world are learning that the ecological crisis is as much about saving children as it is about saving whales.

From U.S. Christian critiques of environmental racism (the targeting of toxic waste sites in poor minority neighborhoods) and Hindu support of the Chipko "tree-hugging" movement in India, to the Engaged Buddhist resistance to nuclear power, world religions are realizing that the ecological crisis runs along the same fault lines as social, political, economic, racial, and gendered oppression.

In the United States, the National Religious Partnership for the Environment provides a salient expression of such religious ecological involvement. The partnership was spawned in 1991 by "An Open Letter to the Religious Community" signed by 32 Nobel laureates and other eminent scientists, including Carl Sagan, Freeman Dyson, and Stephen Jay Gould, among others, inviting the world's religions to take the ecological destruction seriously. Formally established in New York in 1993, the Partnership includes the United States Catholic Conference, the Evangelical Environmental Network, the Coalition on Environment and Jewish Life, and the National Council of Churches of Christ, which, all told, serve more than 100 million U.S. citizens. According to its mission statement, "The Partnership seeks to weave care for God's creation throughout religious life in such a way as to provide inspiration, moral vision, and commitment to social justice for all efforts to protect the natural world and human well-being within it."[3]

Another landmark on the religion-ecology journey is the 10-part, 3-year Harvard Conference on World Religions and Ecology, spearheaded by Mary Evelyn Tucker and John Grim of Yale University. These conferences, organized by the Center for the Study of World Religions at Harvard University, Bucknell University, and the Center for the Respect of Life and Environment, brought together leading scholars and activists from 10 major religious traditions. The Harvard gatherings helped telescope eco-issues for a wide swath of intercellular religious leaders, with the proceedings from the conference being published by the Harvard University Center for the Study of World Religions and Harvard University Press.

Whereas eco-activism is being waged by religious traditions worldwide, as intimated, another critical, unique way religions are dealing with this is through their respective cosmologies.

Scientifically, cosmology entails discerning the laws of the universe and viewing it as an ordered whole. Philosophically, as a branch of metaphysics, cosmology examines the provenance and progression of the created world and the role of the human within it.

Religiously, cosmology also explores the origins of and human place within the universe, yet it views the cosmos as a sacred space and strives to articulate the overarching goal of society, as well as the organizing principles, motivating power, and ultimate purpose or *telos* of our lives.

In pondering these questions, "geologian" Thomas Berry, a Roman Catholic priest enchanted by the awe-inspiring mystery of cosmos, has claimed that the emerging universe should be our basic cosmological framework. This has been eclipsed, he claims, by another cosmology: consumerism.

Using a cultural and scientific lens rather than sociological or economic analysis, Berry avers that rather than viewing the universe as a "communion of subjects," as many religious traditions traditionally have, a consumerist cosmology sees it as a "collection of objects."

What is our role here? To acquire as much "stuff" as possible. What is the goal of society? To have the highest level of mass consumption attainable. Why did God make you? So I can enter the cash-based consumer economy and be competitive in the global marketplace. Consumerism has become our new catechism.

For Berry, the awesome delight of a magnificent sunset or the sense of wonder we feel when gazing at an array of stars on a soft summer night are the sources of the physic energy, the affective power, needed to extricate ourselves from our pathological quest to consume and deface the natural world. Yet these experiences are being increasingly rendered unattainable as pollution smears our twilight horizon and the ever-increasing urban and suburban glare white out our evening skies. (It was claimed that during a major blackout in Los Angeles several years ago, police received dozens of calls from citizens reporting strange lights in the night sky; it was the first time they had seen stars.)

This supplanting of access to the cosmos is also evident in Toronto, Canada's largest city. For years, the McLaughlin Planetarium of the Royal Ontario Museum provided a space where young and old could see an image of the Milky Way galaxy, learn about the origin and progression of the cosmos, fall asleep staring at the simulated planets, and dream cosmic dreams.

Several years ago, this window onto the universe was closed, temporarily replaced by the Kellogg's/IKEA Children's Own Museum. During this time, instead of reaching for the stars in a darkened dome, children spin the corporate logos of IKEA and Kellogg's in the fluorescent-bulbed foyer. Where once they could let their imaginations soar to the beginning of time, children trotted toward a tactile relationship with corporate logos.

In reflecting on our own cosmological frameworks, we are, as a university community, in a uniquely privileged position to reflect on the sounds that fill our lives, the dreams we choose to build, the cosmologies we choose to embrace. All of us, however, share this pivotal time. As Thomas Berry wrote in *Befriending the Earth*,

What is happening in our times is not just another historical transition or simply another cultural change. The devastation of the planet that we are bringing about is negating some hundreds of millions, even billions, of years of past development on the earth. This is a most momentous period of change ...

All indications suggest that we are, in a sense, a chosen group, a chosen generation ...

We did not ask to be here at this time ... Some of the prophets, when asked to undertake certain missions, said, "Don't choose me. That's too much for me." God says, "You are going anyway." We are not asked whether we wish to live at this particular time—we are here. The inescapable is before us.[4]

Poor Bear Burden
of Environmental Hazards

In his compelling work *Amazing Grace: The Lives of Children and the Conscience of a Nation,* social critic Jonathan Kozol interviews children and adults in the Mott Haven section of the South Bronx.

It's one of the poorest congressional districts in the United States and an area with alarmingly high incidences of murder, drug abuse, and poverty. (It is usually not a stop on the Disney – Times Square package tours of the Big Apple.)

Unfortunately, this section of New York also has one of the highest rates of asthma in the nation, and children with inhalers are commonplace. One of the main reasons for the soaring asthma rates, according to Kozol, is the medical waste incinerator operating in the neighbourhood.

Kozol learned from a local minister, Rev. Martha Overall, that the waste incinerator handles so-called red bag products—amputated limbs, fetal tissue, bedding, syringes, and bandages from 14 New York City hospitals. Some of these items were slated to be burned at a proposed incinerator on the East Side of Manhattan, but the proposal was successfully blocked by area parents worried about the cancer risks an incinerator posed for their children.

For both Kozol and Rev. Overall, the ultimate home for this incinerator, in a severely depressed area largely of black and minority residents, is no accident. It is rather an example of what U.S. church groups have labelled "environmental racism."

The term was first used in 1982 by then-director of the United Church of Christ's Commission for Racial Justice, Rev. Ben Chavis. The toxic waste dumps and landfills planned for Warren County, Virginia, a poor, predominantly black community, prompted Chavis to conclude that county was selected for this baleful detritus principally because it was African-American.

As University of Southern Illinois researcher Alison Crane has documented, African-Americans, Hispanics, native Americans, Asians, and other minorities such as migrant workers and the working poor disproportionately suffer harmful health and safety effects as a result of their exposure to various environmental hazards located near their communities. These contamination sources include toxic municipal landfills, waste incinerators, industrial dumps, chemical plants, and uranium mines. (As they say in the real estate trade, the three most important factors in determining property value are location, location, location.)

Today, in the U.S., three out of five black and Hispanic Americans live in communities with one or more toxic waste sites, and more than 15 million African-Americans, more than 8 million Hispanics and about 50 percent of Asian/Pacific Islanders and native Americans are living in communities with one or more abandoned or unsecured toxic waste sites.

A 1987 landmark study conducted by the United Church of Christ's Commission for Racial Justice titled "Toxic Wastes and Race in the United States" documented the extent to which environmental racism affects people of colour, and helped launch the idea of "eco-justice."

According to Joy Kennedy, ecological justice co-ordinator for Kairos, the Canadian Ecumenical Justice Initiative, environmental justice issues in the Canadian context are often related to aboriginal land and treaty concerns.

"Since these issues have not yet been resolved, they, in fact, for aboriginal people, touch on their very identity and status," Kennedy said in a recent interview.

"We don't really call it environmental racism in Canada," Kennedy noted. "It is a different order than racism. It's more about nation and autonomy" for the aboriginal communities.

"To work on environmental issues, it's always local and global—it is one planet."

When addressing global ecological issues such as climate change, however, Canadian churches do take a special interest in how the poor and vulnerable suffer most egregiously from ecological destruction. South Pacific Islanders, African coastal dwellers, and other groups are extremely vulnerable to rising waters from polar ice cap melting and flooding, for example, and experience climate change differently from some sectors of white North Americans who have resources to help insulate them from the most fulsome effects of climate change.

For Kennedy, there is a sense that we in North America feel we can "produce greenhouse gases with impunity," as evinced by the current Canadian government's refusal to meet the requirements of Kyoto.

What analysis of environmental racism does make clear is that the so-called environmental movement is not just the purview of affluent, liberal-minded white North Americans.

The environmental crisis runs along the same fault lines of economic, racial, and political oppression that pockmark our global village. Also, it appears that ecological integrity and racial and economic justice are more deeply intertwined than we ever imagined.

Truth, Lies, and Broadcasting in Canada

A recent, little-noticed news item may result in a deep and indelible blemish on the Canadian mosaic.

Earlier in January 2011, the Canadian Radio-television Telecommunications Commission (CRTC), without fanfare, posted on its website a potential game-changer in the world of broadcast journalism. The CRTC is seeking to relax restrictions concerning the broadcasting of specious information on radio and television.

Currently, the law stipulates that broadcasters "shall not broadcast any false or misleading news."

Sounds reasonable enough—and straightforward—as it should, since it concerns the integrity of news reporting.

But not apparently to the CRTC. It is proposing to soften the regulation banning "any news that the licensee knows is false or misleading and that endangers or is likely to endanger the lives, health or safety of the public."

In short, with the new wording, broadcasters could air false or misleading news with impunity, provided that it does not endanger the lives, health, or safety of the public.

Unfortunately, the CRTC does not specify who will judge whether or not such disinformation poses a danger.

An aphorism comes to mind: "If it's fixed, break it."

The CRTC is apparently responding to concerns raised by Parliament's standing joint committee for the scrutiny of regulations, which worried that such a sweeping ban may not withstand a court challenge under the Charter of Rights.

It seems, however, that the societal benefits of a commitment to truth-telling in broadcasting far outweigh any potential legal potholes emerging with a hypothetical court case in future.

As University of Ottawa law professor and media expert Michael Geist points out, there is some irony in the CRTC's timing. Just as the U.S., reeling from the Arizona massacre that targeted Democratic Congresswoman Gabrielle Giffords, is reflecting on the wider social impact of its poisoned airwaves, the CRTC is embracing a more U.S.-style approach.

This is made all the more disconcerting as a new right-leaning all-news network, Sun TV News, prepares for its debut in March. In a recent interview, Geist observed there's a growing fear that Canada is about to adopt the more bellicose U.S. approach to political news coverage. The CRTC's proposed change will only deepen these fears.

"I think that those same kinds of fears are out there in much the same way [as they are in the U.S.]. This just provides freer licence to do it," Geist commented.

Yet concerns over journalistic integrity in Canada are not new. Over the past 15 years, many have sounded warnings, and some of the clearest and most compelling tocsins have been rung by the venerable dean of Canadian journalists, Knowlton Nash.

The former anchorman for CBC's *The National,* with more than half a century's experience in print and broadcast journalism, Nash laments the obsession of the media with the pursuit of "trivia," as well as its increasing preoccupation with "entertainment and gossip" at the expense of well-grounded analysis and truly investigative reporting.

In his book, *Trivia Pursuit: How Showbiz Values Are Corrupting the News* (1998), Nash sees the "dumbing down" of the news and the supplanting of crucial political events by celebrity scuttlebutt as nothing less than a threat to Canadian democracy.

In a series of lectures he once graciously delivered to my under-graduate students, Nash noted that when serving as an "unembedded" CBC journalist during the war in Vietnam, he was with a U.S. platoon as it engaged in a firefight. He saw several U.S. troops killed.

When he attended the official U.S. military briefing later that afternoon, however, a U.S. army media official stated unequivocally that there had been "no casualties" that day. (There was a reason journalists called those official afternoon briefings the "five o'clock follies.")

For Nash, while the full truth of any situation will always at some level elude us, the commitment to truth-telling, which was a hallmark of his journalism career, should never be watered down.

The importance of such a commitment cannot be overstated; for any "news" that deliberately misleads can only be the product of a society that is seriously misguided.

The Ecological Crisis

*Reason says that
destroying clean air is
impractical;
faith ought to say it is
blasphemous.*

Joseph Sittler

The above epigraph represents both a horizon and a hope. As a pioneering Christian theological voice, Joseph Sittler, in 1961, articulated the need for a theology of the environment, one that took the destruction of the natural world at human hands as a sign, not of progress, or advancement, but of ecological and spiritual crisis.[1]

Since then, a growing crescendo of Christian voices has been raised in a defense of nature, especially resonant after cultural historian Lynn White's 1967 polemic, which claimed that the Judeo-Christian tradition's anthropocentric roots had laid the cultural foundations for the environmental crisis.[2] The Christian responses to this charge have consequently explored the need for a Christian ecological theology, and helped spawn an emerging body of Christian organizations, reflection, and social teaching dedicated to stewardship and environmental sustainability.

Yet there is not a consensus in the Christian world, as yet, surrounding Sittler's injunction to label pollution blasphemous. The wedding of modern Christianity with modern social and economic movements, in which nature was the canvas on which the human and Christian spirit painted its dreams, is presently being challenged by a plethora of theologians, philosophers, scientists, and environmentalists, and the role of the human—and indeed the vocation of the Christian—lies in the balance. The understanding of the human artisan and of God's artistry in nature is being radically reviewed, and our relationship to the "canvas" of nature is being deeply questioned.

The environmental signs are quite distressing as a new millennium dawns. From the polar ice caps to the remote depths of the Pacific Ocean, evidence of human-engendered pollutants can now be found. We are experiencing a rate of species extinction, estimated by some at 17 species of flora and fauna a day, unprecedented since the dinosaur age closed with a bang or a whimper (scientists aren't sure which) some 65 million years ago. Greenhouse gases, according to a plurality of the world's climate experts, are generating a dramatic warming effect upon the world, leading to wide swings in weather patterns, flooding, and other natural disasters of seemingly apocalyptic proportions. Indeed, 1998 was deemed the hottest year on record, and most of the leading contenders for that ominous honor have been in the 1990s.[3] Consumerism and militarization continue throughout the Northern nations and increasingly permeate nations of the South, while countries such as China rapidly replace salutary bicycles for non – emissions tested automobiles at a disturbing rate.

Deforestation, especially among tropical rainforests, is occurring at the rate of one football field a second—an area the size of Austria— each year. Moreover, according to the United Nations, 35,000 children die daily owing to diseases engendered by contaminated water and food, and the growth of the human family will reach 6 billion, it is estimated, shortly into the 21st century. (As such a litany attests, one could convincingly argue that ecology now rivals economics as "the gloomy science."[4])

While the 20th century certainly did not have a monopoly on environmental destruction or concern for nature, philosophically, theologically, or practically speaking, it did witness several significant, distinctive environmental moments which are worth exploring here.

Moment One: The Dawn of the Environmental Movement

Rachel Carson: Recasting Our Relationship with Nature

While Joseph Sittler was sounding a tocsin for nature amid hallowed theological halls, Rachel Carson, a biologist, writer, and former editor-in-chief of the U.S. Fish and Wildlife Service, rang an environmental alarm that reverberated throughout the corridors of U.S. corporate and political power. Having achieved critical and financial success with *The Sea Around Us*,[5] which settled comfortably for weeks on *The New York Times* bestseller list, Carson in 1962 launched her most influential book, *Silent Spring*, which many claim to be the single most important event in alerting the world to the hazards of environmental poisoning by pesticides, or "biocides," as she termed them. Attacked by chemical companies and threatened with legal action from powerful interests (as were *The New Yorker* and Houghton-Mifflin for publishing her work), Carson, valiantly fighting breast cancer, persevered with her project. Once published, *Silent Spring* became an immediate bestseller, sparking hearings in the U.S. Senate and a presidential report from the Kennedy administration resulting in a ban on DDT use in the United States.[6]

Carson argued that for humanity to think it can somehow transcend the laws of nature is equivalent to thinking it can repeal the law of gravity. In contradistinction to the reigning sense that humans were "at war with nature" and, in particular, with "hordes of insects" that jeopardized crops and hence human survival, Carson pushed for organic alternatives to pest control in keeping with natural processes.

Sadly observing that the "current vogue for poisons" demonstrated "no humility" before the fabric of nature—"a fabric on the one hand delicate and destructible, on the other miraculously tough and resilient"—Carson wrote in *Silent Spring*:

> The "control of nature" is a phrase conceived in arrogance, born of the Neanderthal age of biology and philosophy, when

it was supposed that nature exists for the convenience of man. The concepts and practices of applied entomology for the most part date from that Stone Age of science. It is our alarming misfortune that so primitive a science has armed itself with the most modern and terrible weapons, and that in turning them against the insects it has also turned them against the earth.[7]

While Carson is generally regarded as the fountainhead of the modern environmental movement, her antecedents are many: Henry David Thoreau, the civilly disobedient naturalist and author of *Walden*; John Muir, founder of the Sierra Club and chief protagonist for the establishment of Yosemite National Park; Aldo Leopold, a visionary conservationist whose *A Sand County Almanac* is the first seedling of environmental ethics; and Albert Schweitzer, who developed an ethic of "reverence for life" as a sustainable leitmotif amid the rubble and smog of the post–World War II period, and to whom Rachel Carson dedicated *Silent Spring*.[8]

Moment Two: Environmental Destruction as a Theological Concern

Lynn White Jr. and the Advent of Ecological Theology

Though Joseph Sittler had been calling for a serious and sustained theological reflection on the environment in the early 1960s, it was not until 1967, with the publication of Lynn White's accusatory article "The Historical Roots of Our Ecologic Crisis," that Christian theologians were impelled to deal with the environmental onslaught and their own culpability for the crisis.

A cultural historian and practicing Christian, White asserted that Christianity is the "most anthropocentric religion" the world has ever known. Though observing countervailing trends in the writings of St. Francis of Assisi, whom White nominated as patron saint of ecology (a designation later affirmed by Pope John Paul II), White claimed that the Judeo-Christian tradition on the whole, owing to its sense of the human as a subduer of the Earth with a divine injunction to have dominion over creation, provided the moral, cultural, and spiritual foundation for the birth of aggressive and environmentally harmful technologies. Why did the scratch plow first emerge in medieval Europe rather than in the great civilizations of Persia or China? For White, one need go no further than the focus on human power and redemption inherent in Western Christianity.

White's critique was perhaps meant more as a gauntlet thrown before the tradition than a Molotov cocktail tossed within it. Nevertheless, coming as it did in the late 1960s, with an emerging cultural critique of traditional political, educational, and religious traditions, White's thesis was waved broadly by the secular environmental movement in North America, eager to distance itself from a tradition often seen more as a keeper of the status quo than as a force for progressive change. Consequently, the budding environmental movement did not readily embrace an alliance with members of one of the most effective shapers of public consciousness and action in North America, that is, the mainline Christian churches.[9]

In theological circles White's article promoted an explosion of articles and books, leading him jocularly to refer to himself as the "founder of ecological theology."[10] In the aftermath of his challenge, Christian responses adopted three main positions.[11]

First, there is what might be termed the "apologetic" or defensive response, which avers that White had insufficient biblical background or understanding of the nuances of the Christian tradition to support his statements. These responses cull from biblical scholarship and church tradition in order to defend the Judeo-Christian legacy from White's charges. They also suggest that the emergence of Western technology was a complex and multi-branched phenomenon, one that could not be facilely attributed to a single root cause. Among the most prominent of these spokespersons are philosopher Robin Attfield and theologians Thomas Sieger Derr and H. Paul Santmire;[12] Santmire's *Travail of Nature* painstakingly pours the sands of the Christian tradition through an ecological sieve, finding two parallel movements, one "spiritual" and the other "ecological," with the latter providing the seeds, Santmire claims, for a positive theology of the environment.

The constructive position, the second response, acknowledges that environmental concerns were not at the forefront of theology. While conceding that it had been a while since they last heard a sermon on safeguarding the non-human world, many in this camp intimate that there are fruits in the tradition that can be harvested, and their seeds cultivated, for a more sanguine response to nature. Theologian Douglas John Hall,[13] who explores Christian dominion as a form of stewardship, and Jürgen Moltmann,[14] who delineates an ecological doctrine of creation from a trinitarian perspective, are but two architects of this approach. The pioneering work of John B. Cobb Jr., Jay B. McDaniel, and Catherine Keller, through the lens of process theology, has attempted to see the interconnection of the human with the non-human in dialogue with contemporary physics, economics, and animal-rights literature.

Ecofeminism, which relates the oppression of women to the domination of nature, strives to move from a cultural paradigm of patriarchy to one of mutuality and builds on a critical theological response to social injustice and sexism. Rosemary Radford Ruether, Sallie McFague, Heather Eaton, and physicist Vandana Shiva represent important voices in this emergent literature.[15] In addition, the nascent Latin American social ecology of Leonardo Boff and Ivone Gebara is also representative of this creative engagement with the Christian tradition in light of environmental degradation, claiming that the same cultural, political, and economic forces that render the majority of the world's peoples destitute are also rapaciously destroying the world's ecosystems.[16]

A third response to White, the "listening approach," in many ways transcends the debate, suggesting that Christianity has to listen to science, other religious traditions, and nature itself to get its bearing in a sea of environmental peril. Among the spokespersons here are Thomas Berry and his former students John Grim and Mary Evelyn Tucker. The work of Thomas Berry, a self-dubbed "geologian," is noteworthy as much for its progression as for its content. A cultural historian and Passionist priest who once served in China, Berry founded a center for world religions at Fordham University in New York, the first such center at a Catholic institution, and published important texts in the areas of Buddhism and Eastern thought.

Arguably, however, his most lasting work has come since 1970, when he established the Riverdale Center for Religious Research and published his papers on the "new cosmology." Though circulated among friends and members of the American Teilhard Association for years, they were not published in book form until the *Dream of the Earth* appeared.[17] Berry, once a "lone voice for the wilderness," is now seen as one of the progenitors of the modern religious environmental movement, and his advice was sought by U.S. President Bill Clinton; Vice-President Al Gore; the U.S. bishops; and church, civic, and educational leaders around the world. Interestingly, recognition of the importance of Berry's work has grown concomitantly with interest in Christian circles in the environmental crisis. Thomas Berry, a humble and prescient priest from the red hills of North Carolina, though deceased, serves as an intellectual grandfather and inspiration to several generations of religious and spiritual seekers of environmental sustainability, including many women religious congregations whose practical ecoministries combine Berry's thought with pragmatic acts of social justice.

Indeed, the spill of books, papers, conferences, and organizations around environmental issues in the Christian world has been sizable, from the National Religious Partnership on the Environment to the Harvard Conference on World Religions and Ecology spearheaded by Mary Evelyn Tucker (1998), the increasing environmental focus by the National Catholic Rural Life Conference, the Center for Respect of Life and the Environment, the North American Coalition on Religion for Ecology, and many others.[18] The formation of such groups has been accompanied by an increasing volume of the Catholic social teaching on the environment, from Pope John Paul II's 1990 World Day of Peace message, the first to focus on ecological concerns, to environmental statements from bishops' conferences in the Philippines, Dominican Republic, United States, Canada, and elsewhere. There has been tremendous growth in awareness and action from Christian theological voices around the environment.[19]

Moment Three: The Commingling of Social Justice and Environmental Concerns

Toward a Political Theology of the Environment

Intriguingly, the environmental consciousness of Christian churches was being prodded by Lynn White just as its social conscience was also being tweaked by liberation theologians.[20] Just as liberation theologians were developing a preferential option for the poor, and a critique of economic, social, and military structures that continue to lock generations of people in Southern nations in the iron grip of misery, environmental theologians were also attempting to chart a new ground for theology. They sought a new context—not only social and political but also environmental.

For many years the connections between these two views, social justice and ecology, were not readily discerned. At one gathering at the College Theology Society in Loyola Marymount University in Los Angeles, Thomas Berry and Jon Sobrino, S.J., from El Salvador, author of *Christology at the Crossroads* (1978) and leading liberation theologian, sat together on a panel, but their worldviews remained in different places. Frustrated with Berry's presentation, Sobrino at one point wondered how Berry could equate the life of a starving child with that of a bird. Berry, on his part, noting the absence of Christian reflection on eco-destruction, was critical of certain biblical approaches to the environmental movement. He would observe later that Christians should "put the Bible on the shelf for twenty years and listen to nature."[21]

Fortunately, a confluence of sorts has begun between these two important theological streams. Leonardo Boff, the famous Brazilian liberation theologian twice silenced by the Vatican for his views, has sought to integrate a preferential option for the poor with a preferential option for the Earth. He has drawn a compelling connection between environmental and human rights concerns especially in the area of indigenous cultures of the Amazon rainforest, where a way of life is being torched along with the rainforest itself.[22] With Mary Evelyn Tucker and John Grim, Boff has served as editor of the Ecology and Justice series of Orbis Books, the premier publisher of liberation theology. Moreover, churches have looked increasingly at environmental racism in North America and elsewhere as both a social justice and an ecological issue. With the aid of the social sciences, church groups are realizing it is no accident that toxic waste dumps and noxious, poison-spewing incinerators are located in poorer neighborhoods in the United States, often where a majority of the citizens are black or Hispanic. (Intriguingly, Jon Sobrino currently comments on the need of a theology of creation, and Thomas Berry acknowledged that his work is vulnerable to social-injustice critiques.)

It is increasingly evident that environmental issues run along the same fissures that mark our social and political landscape. While interconnections were articulated, as mentioned, by theologians such as Joseph Sittler and Rosemary Radford Ruether, they were made institutionally in the 1970s by the World Council of Churches' Justice, Peace, and Integrity of Creation Initiative, which saw all three concerns as interrelated.

In many ways the melding of political theology and ecological religious reflection is among the most promising and hope-yielding theological developments at the crepuscule of the 20th century. Such a convergence points out the need for an integrated response to both human suffering and environmental destruction, a chord sounded strongly in the Jubilee statements of progressive Christian coalitions worldwide, who invoke the biblical tradition in Deuteronomy of every fifty years forgiving debts, giving the land a rest, and releasing slaves. The Canadian Ecumenical Jubilee Initiative, in particular, has stressed these three dimensions of Jubilee in terms of debt cancelation for Southern nations, release of persons sold into prostitution and child labor rings, and protecting the environment. These are sanguine millennium resolutions, as it were.

Yet there is a growing need for the churches and theologians to take the environmental crisis seriously. Here, we can all benefit from the example of religious women who have done environmental audits of their property, supported women religious in full-time environmental ministry, sponsored community-supported organic agriculture, and led education programs influenced by the new cosmology of Brian

Swimme and Thomas Berry, which link social justice with a love for creation. They are practitioners of a new type of political theology, an ecological theology of politics, as it were, that sees the context of theology with new eyes—not just human, but non-human as well. Such a theology will have to take seriously the tendency toward anthropocentrism in the tradition. It must develop what I have termed elsewhere an "anthro-harmonic approach," with harmonic suggesting "of an integrated nature."[23] This perspective views the human in a mutually constitutive relationship with creation, not simply as lord and master over it. It intimates that while the human has a unique potency to both wreck and restore creation, the human is also in some ways dependent on creation for moral, spiritual, and physical well-being. In this sense, human and non-human nature share a "dialectical contingency," a fundamental integration, which must form the context for theological exploration. Just as we are not above nature, so too are we not at its service. Our biblical tradition calls us to a special concern for the systematically impoverished and destitute, and to use the fruits of our science to bring about not only a just society, but a sustainable one, where the gifts of the Creator are preserved not simply in gated communities for the affluent but in the open garden of creation, our home.

Questions to Ponder
and Exercises to Consider

1. In "The Ecological Crisis," Scharper asks us to think of a place in nature that was special to us and whether it still exists today. *Why* was it special to you? Consider Richard Louv's notion of "nature deficit disorder." What benefits do you see in encouraging children—and adults, for that matter—to get out of their houses to spend more time in nature?

2. Related to the question above, try this exercise that he assigns to his Introduction to Environment class: go 24 hours unplugged and spend at least three of those hours in nature. This means going a whole day without your computer, cellphone, iPod, tablet, music player, TV, and even your e-reader. After the period is over, note the experience. Did you manage to stay away from tweeting or texting someone for the whole time? What did you do in its place? Whether or not you were successful in disconnecting from the e-world, how did the experience make you feel?

3. Environmental racism is discussed in a couple of readings in this section. Have you considered whether there is environmental racism happening in your locality? It's not hard to figure out. Get hold of a map of your city or town or region. Mark the areas where most of the industries, factories, or civic waste management sites are located. Then mark the areas where you find the greatest levels of poverty (the websites of a number of government offices or non-government social or environmental organizations can supply you

with much of this information). Once you have done this, mark the areas on the same map where you might find the largest percentage of health issues related to breathing (asthma, for instance), heart disease or cancer (again, the website or office of a local or regional health centre or non-profit health association can help you here). What, if any, pattern(s) did you find? In which section of the map do you live?

4. In "The Ecological Crisis," Scharper discusses the uneasy process of reconciling social justice and ecological issues. He mentions how one liberation theologian, Jon Sobrino, becomes frustrated with Thomas Berry, wondering how "Berry could equate the life of a starving child to that of a bird." Equally frustrated, Berry criticizes the "absence of Christian reflection on eco-destruction" and of "biblical approaches to the environmental movement." In both instances, these Christians are discussing values: the value of the human to that of the non-human. How do you value each? Do you share the frustrations of either Sobrino or Berry?

SECTION II

Reflecting—What on Earth Are We Doing?

Introduction

It used to be said humans were at war with nature.
Now that we are "winning" this war,
the heinous price of victory
is becoming tragically apparent.

Stephen Bede Scharper

Continuing his reflection on the human's role in destroying flourishing ecosystems of the planet and directly changing the course of geological history, Scharper in this section is compelled to ask, "What on Earth are we doing?" This question, in turn, raises the more fundamental question that Scharper begins to explore in more·detail: What is our role as humans on Earth?

By exploring the scientific, philosophical, and theological under-standings of the Gaia theory, ecofeminism, and liberation theology, Scharper explores novel ways of being in and understanding our world. He proceeds thoughtfully so that no essential wisdom from our past is overlooked, nor any new or old notion naively incorporated; this is what is meant by "reflecting." In this way, he concludes that the Gaia theory can provide us with a suitable framework for articulating the role of the human within a social justice perspective, but *not* without the inclusion of the social, political, and economic dimensions that underpin our ecological crises, as put forth by ecofeminists and libera-tion theologians. Ultimately, in this section Scharper begins to build a framework for the development of a new human/non-human rela-tionship, which is discussed in even more detail in the third section.

Readers will note that Scharper refers to his method of exploration as a "political theology of the environment" approach. As discussed in the introduction to this book, this method entails examining one's faith and worldview from the perspectives of those struggling for dignity, seeking freedom from sexism and economic oppression, and working toward ecological sustainability for the entire planet. Moreover, the oppressed, alienated, and suffering of our world are not just human, but other-than-human as well. A political theology of the environment approach is a down-to-Earth way of looking at our entire planet, with the human subject as an integral component, in a manner that is self-critical and is open to a range of insights, models, and ways of knowing the world. It is a comprehensive methodology that, by the end of this book, should become more familiar to you.

Deep ecology, which is mentioned throughout this section, serves as a good example of how Scharper's political theology of the environment approach comes into play. Deep ecology represents an ecological worldview that recognizes the inherent worth of all living things—their *intrinsic* value. The phrase "deep ecology" was coined by Norwegian philosopher Arne Naess in 1973. Naess underlines that the value of non-human life forms must be seen as independent of the usefulness these may have for narrow human purposes. In fact, an important principle of deep ecology asserts that humans have no right to reduce the richness and diversity of life on this planet to mere instruments of human agendas. For this reason, it is considered a radically non-anthropocentric way of thinking. In contrast to deep ecology lies what some call *shallow environmental thinking*, or *instrumentalist thinking*. This thinking is strongly anthropocentric, since the value of things in nature is determined by their significance to fulfilling human needs.

Not surprisingly, given our global ecological situation, deep ecology has gained much attention and favour in the past few decades among environmental activists and thinkers. To some, it offers a spirituality that fosters Earthly, even cosmic, unity. Such a way of thinking suggests that human fulfillment can come about only by identifying with the entire universe. While not eschewing its merit for demonstrating our spiritual and physical interconnectedness to creation, Scharper rejects deep ecology's understandings of the human as being somewhat insignificant. As the first short article in this section suggests, deep ecology fails at times to take that crucial and critical look in the same mirror that confronted Scharper when he visited New York's Bronx Zoo when he was a child. He notes that the sign above the mirror boldly stated, "You are looking at the most dangerous animal in the world."

With this mirror test in mind, then, it becomes clear that when discussing the role of the human on Earth, neither the anthropocentric nor the radically non-anthropocentric view will do.

We All Lose in the War Against Nature

I remember as a child visiting New York's Bronx Zoo. After marvelling at the human-eating lions and fierce-toothed bears, I was confronted by a mirror. The sign above boldly stated, "You are looking at the most dangerous animal in the world." It was an unsettling message for a 10-year-old.

A similar mirror was recently held up to the entire human family by scientists writing in the journal *Environmental Science & Technology*, who claim that, through wanton destruction of species and significant alteration of the planet's climate, humans are ushering in a new geological era, "the Anthropocene." For the first time in the Earth's history, humans are in the driver's seat of geological evolution. Through rapid urbanization, widespread pollution, skyrocketing population, rapacious mining, and the excessive combustion of fossil fuels, we are bringing in a new and disconcerting dawn of geological history, one that may entail the sixth largest mass extinction the world has ever witnessed.

It used to be said humans were at war with nature. Now that we are "winning" this war, the heinous price of victory is becoming tragically apparent.

While this item was not front-page news, it might prove to be one of the most important and memorable stories of our time, indeed, of all time—literally.

Nobel laureate Paul Crutzen of the Max Planck Institute for Chemistry, one of the authors of the article, first raised this notion of the Anthropocene epoch a decade ago, and it has since gained increasing acceptance within geological circles. So much so that the International Union of Geological Sciences may within the next few years officially decide on whether such a transition has indeed occurred.

The idea that humans are at the control panel of the Earth's geology, however, has more than scientific resonance. More than 20 years ago, cultural historian and Roman Catholic priest Thomas Berry, reflecting on our current state of mass extinctions, said that humans were closing down the last 65 million years of life on the planet, the Cenozoic era, the "lyrical" period which gave us mammals and flowers. For Berry, though, we have a choice concerning our new geological future. It could be more of the same, leading to what he called a "Technozoic" era, rendering our planet a "wasteworld," or we could move to an "Ecozoic" period, developing economies and technologies that seek to work with, rather than against, the life systems of the planet and help effect a "wonderworld."

Berry challenges our cultural and religious institutions to take this historical moment seriously. While all religious traditions reflect on the proper role of the human within nature, the Anthropocene moment recasts this question in an unprecedented way. We are the first generation to be able to close down the magnificent, flourishing ecosystems of the planet and directly change the course of geological history.

Acknowledging this capacity is only part of the challenge. What we as a society are compelled to ask is: "What on Earth are we doing?" With such a capacity, what special responsibilities do we as a human community now assume?

What cultural, civic, environmental, spiritual, and religious values are fostering our destructive activities, and which can be embraced to help chart a more sustainable future?

These are but a few questions to ponder as we, as a species, face ourselves in the mirror.

O Ye of Little Eco-faith

And this our life ...
Finds tongues in trees, books in the running brooks,
Sermons in stones, and good in everything.

William Shakespeare, *As You Like It*

My religion is rain.

Drew Dellinger, *A Hymn to the Sacred Body of the Universe*

*I*s environmentalism a new religion? *This question, recently posed by the effervescent Shelagh Rogers on CBC Radio One, is both timely and intriguing.*

Timely because of the current surge in eco-interest, owing in no small measure to Al Gore's *An Inconvenient Truth*, a cinematic splash of melted polar ice-cap water on a population in denial of global warming.

Intriguing, because it highlights the compelling spiritual allure of the environmental movement, especially for young people, and the challenge it poses to mainstream religions.

But is it really a religion?

The Latin origins of the word are varied. *Religio* denotes respect for what is sacred. The term is also related to *relegere*, which means "to read again," and was apparently also influenced in the popular ancient imagination by *religare*, which means "to bind" as in the sense "to place an obligation on."

While religion speaks of people's beliefs and opinions concerning the existence, nature, and worship of a deity or deities, and an institutionalized codification of those beliefs in doctrine, rituals, and practices, it also can mean a set of strongly held beliefs, values, and attitudes that somebody lives by.

This latter meaning is perhaps the type of environmental "religion" held by 20 percent of Canadians identified in a recent Tory government report. Cynically dubbed the "Suzuki Nation" after the famed Canadian environmentalist, this group, according to the report, finds the degraded state of the environment an affront to their values. They are thus motivated to take environmental action even without the carrots of tax breaks and other monetary incentives.

It seems that even the Tories are among those wondering if environmentalism is a new religion. And the fact that anti-environmental political groups are suddenly sprouting green tendrils points to the profound rereading of our life and culture spawned by our ecological profligacy.

Ecological concerns appear to have, particularly in the past year, permeated most parts of our collective consciousness. Climate change, rapid species extinction, poisoned air, polluted water systems, tropical forest burning, rampant militarism, ozone depletion, toxic waste sites—all have begun to make steady headline copy in the media, and raise profound questions for our culture.

Our current ecological moment is so grave and on such a profound scale that it compels us to rethink the basic question of what it means to be human. This touches us at the core of our being, a being that is not only rational but psychological, emotional, phenomenological, and, indeed, spiritual.

As we slow cook our climate with fossil fuel emissions, delete thousands of species annually, cut down our remaining old growth forests, and watch as thousands of children die owing to contaminated water, we are confronted with sobering questions, questions of a deeply philosophical and spiritual vintage.

What is our role here? What is the vocation of the human as a species? What kind of world do we wish to leave future generations? What is the goal of "civilization" if its thrust forward leaves behind the world's ecosystems, a vast swath of the animal species as veritable roadkill? What on Earth are we doing?

Our perceived role as master and lord over nature, which in some cases has ancient religious wellsprings but was given a hefty leg-up through modern industrialization, is now paired with an increasing sense of our interrelationship with and dependence upon the Earth's natural systems, and with the non-human animals that form an integral part of those systems.

What is our proper place, then, between the rock of our technological prowess and the hard place of our biological vulnerability and profound interconnection with the rest of creation?

All of these questions are critical in coming to grips with the enormity of the ecological challenge before us; they constitute a summons to fashion a new human/non-human relationship. They are ultimately, no matter how we colour and contour them, spiritual and religious questions.

While it is up for grabs whether environmentalism is a new religion, it is clear that environmentalism is new to religion. How religions respond to this eco-challenge may indeed have profound consequences for the face—and fate—of all creation.

The Gaia Theory:
Implications for a Christian Political
Theology of the Environment

Most of us sense that the Earth is more than a sphere of rock
with a thin layer of air, ocean, and life covering the surface.
We feel that we belong here,
as if this planet were indeed our home.
Long ago the Greeks, thinking this way,
gave to the Earth the name of Gaia.

James Lovelock, *The Ages of Gaia*

As competing definitions or understandings of humanity's role in the patterns of ecological sustainability emerge, the place of the human in the world becomes increasingly crucial to explore. The deleterious use of human technology, at the service of industrial capitalism and socialism as well as militarism and consumerism during the modern era, has jeopardized many of the life-systems of the planet. Those interested in a Christian theology of the environment must navigate past the Scylla of an anthropocentric notion of creation in which humanity is seen as the driving, domineering, and superior species, and the Charybdis of a completely non-anthropocentric vision, which would leave to other species the task of cleaning up human environmental destruction, a task for which they appear ill-equipped. A political theology of the environment that utilizes social, economic, and cultural analysis in order to show how human agents may advance a society more in harmony with a gospel vision of a just, peaceful, and sustainable society thus becomes an important field of cultivation in light of the cultural and intellectual tumult spawned by our ecological insensitivity.

There are, of course, myriad frameworks for looking at the role of the human within the environmental crisis. Ecofeminism, environmental ethics, animal-rights advocacy, deep ecology, green politics, and sustainable development are but a handful. The Gaia theory has become another such framework. Gaia is significant because it fuses scientific insight and religious imagination in a potentially energizing and transformative way, challenging persons across a broad spectrum of disciplines to deal in an integrative fashion with the ecological crisis. Moreover, just as the Copernican revolution forced humanity to alter its self-proclaimed centrality within the universe, so may Gaia hold the potential for a similarly foundational cultural transition.

The Gaia Theory: What Is It?

First articulated by British atmospheric chemist James Lovelock as a hypothesis, the Gaia theory succinctly suggests that the Earth is a self-regulating, self-sustaining entity, which continually adjusts its environment in order to support life.[1] Though a *scientific* idea, the Gaia theory has, since its initial articulation in 1969, sparked a swirl of religious, New Age, and philosophical reflection and challenged certain long-held assumptions about evolution, the importance of the human in determining environmental change, and the relationship between life and the environment.

While serving as a consultant for NASA during the 1960s, Lovelock worked on the Viking project, which assayed to determine whether life existed or was even possible on Mars. To probe these questions, Lovelock examined what sustained life on Earth, and, arguing from his strength as an atmospheric chemist, found his answer in the composition of the Earth's atmosphere, with its delicate balance of oxygen, hydrogen, nitrogen, methane, and traces of other elements.[2] In attempting to answer the question of life's existence on Mars, Lovelock concentrated on the nature of the Earth's atmosphere and argued that "the entire range of living matter on Earth, from whales to viruses, from oaks to algae, could be regarded as constituting a single living entity, capable of manipulating the Earth's atmosphere to suit its overall needs and endowed with faculties and powers far beyond those of its constituent parts."[3]

Unlike Mars, with an atmosphere composed mainly of carbon dioxide, the Earth, Lovelock concluded, had a dynamic and self-regulating atmosphere. Just like an oven thermostat that maintains a constant temperature, the Earth's atmosphere sustained a stable balance of gases and temperature supportive of life. Because Mars had no suggestion of such a matrix or dynamic atmosphere, Lovelock concluded, it is lifeless.

For Lovelock, life is not surrounded by a passive environment to which it has accustomed itself. Rather, life creates and reshapes its own environment.[4] Whereas traditional Earth scientists maintain that the Earth's climatic pattern is more geological than biological, and is therefore less robust and more vulnerable to lasting injury, the Gaia thesis purports that the Earth is like a self-regulating animal, and may have organs that are especially important, such as the rainforest and wetlands, which are more vital to the global environment than are other parts of the system.[5] In other words, while Gaia may sustain the loss of its "big toe," i.e., the blue whale, it can ill afford to lose its "lungs," i.e., the tropical rainforests.

One could argue that historical antecedents of the Gaia theory reside in the work of G. F. Hegel, Baruch Spinoza, Alfred North Whitehead, and Herbert Spencer, all of whom spoke of nature in terms of an organism. Moreover, Aldo Leopold, deemed the father of the modern conservation movement, viewed the Earth as an "organism" possessing a certain degree of life. As philosopher Anthony Weston also points out, the Gaia theory has a particular relevance to our time, with its general systems theory and interplanetary expeditions.[6] Evolutionary philosopher Elisabet Sahtouris notes that early in this century, the Russian scientist V. I. Vernadsky viewed the biogeochemistry of the planet as a unity, but his work was not known to Lovelock until after the Gaia thesis was proposed.[7] Lovelock himself points to the 19th-century Scottish scientist James Hutton, the father of geology, as a Gaia forerunner. Hutton spoke of the Earth as a "superorganism," and was one of the first scientists to conceive of the Earth in a systems context.[8]

With the help of the late Lynn Margulis, Lovelock has refined his thesis, and has been able to reinforce his ideas scientifically with reference to Margulis's research on microorganisms. Known amusingly as "The Wizard of Ooze" owing to her investigation of microbes in swamps, mudflats, and marshes around the world, Margulis maintained that symbiosis and cooperation have been as central to biological evolution as has the competitive conflict for survival that marks Darwinian theory.[9]

For Margulis and Sagan, interrelation, rather than competition, is the leitmotif of nature. Like Lovelock, they see the biosphere as "seamless," a grand, integrated, and living organism. They assert that the first bacteria acquired almost all the necessary knowledge about living in an integrated schema. "Life did not take over the globe by combat," they contend, "but by networking."[10] Attempting to show the importance of microorganisms for Gaia, Margulis was quick to demonstrate that life on Earth has existed on the planet for 3.5 billion years, and that for the first 2 billion, only bacterial microorganisms existed. Mammals, including the human, she went on to speculate, may exist solely to provide warm homes for such micro-organisms.[11]

For Bunyard and Goldsmith, co-editors of the British journal *The Ecologist: Journal of the Post-Industrial Age,* the Gaia theory suggests that the biosphere, together with the atmospheric environment, constitute a unified natural system. This system is the fruit of organic forces that are highly coordinated by the system itself. Gaia has, in effect, created herself, not in a random manner, but actually in an objective-seeking fashion. This is suggested by the fact that the system is highly stable and can maintain its equilibrium despite internal and external dilemmas. It is actually a "cybernetic" system and thus must be seen as a grand cooperative project. Bunyard and Goldsmith aver that if "Gaia is a single natural system that has created herself in a coordinated and goal-directed way, then Gaia is clearly the unit of evolution, not the individual living thing as neo-Darwinists insist."[12] In fact, they speculate, Gaia might be evolution itself. Competition becomes not the primary feature, but a secondary one, and survival of the fittest becomes not a highly individualistic exercise, but a cooperative attempt to weed out certain species for the benefit of the organic commonweal. They insist that now there is more evidence for Gaia as an evolutionary process than there is for neo-Darwinism.[13]

While many environmentalists initially warmed to the Gaia theorists, perceiving them to be natural allies in the eco-struggle, Lovelock and Margulis proved to be reluctant eco-partners. One of the reasons for this distancing lies in the minimal place the human holds in the overall Gaia theory as articulated by Lovelock and Margulis. For the Gaia theory originators, Gaia is a self-regulating system, a "creature," which moves forward into the future regardless of what humans do.

In his first full-blown, popular articulation of his theory, *Gaia: A New Look at Life on Earth,* Lovelock clearly distinguishes himself from mainstream environmentalists. In this imaginatively written work, Lovelock asserts that, contrary to the gloomy forecasts of environmentalists, life on Earth is robust, hardy, and extremely adaptable, as his analysis of Gaia regulation over the eons intimates. He suggests that large plants and animals are in fact probably less important than are bacteria deep in soils and seabeds. He compares "higher species," e.g., trees and mammals, to glitzy salesmen and show models used to display products; helpful but not essential. He goes as far as to say that even nuclear war would probably not affect Gaia drastically.[14]

Pollution, for Lovelock, is as natural as are sea and sand, and is therefore not fulsome but simply organic, an inevitable byproduct of "life at work." The early biosphere, he argues, must have experienced pollution and the depletion of resources, as we do in the modern world. He notes that the first entity to use zinc beneficially probably also produced mercury as a poisonous waste product. Microorganisms were later produced to break down the mercury, representing perhaps life's most ancient toxic waste disposal system.[15]

While conceding that the devastation of modern industrial and technological development may prove "destructive and painful" for our own species, Lovelock doubts that it threatens the life of Gaia as a whole. (The ethical questions surrounding the "pain" for the human species are left unexplored.) In fact, he continues, "the very concept of pollution is anthropocentric and it may even be irrelevant in the Gaian context."[16] Acknowledging his lack of concern for the place of humanity within the Gaia framework, Lovelock admits that his work "is not primarily about people and livestock and pets; it is about the biosphere and the magic of Mother Earth."[17]

Yet Lovelock, in ascribing a peripheral role for humanity in the Gaian framework, neglects to take into account socio-economic factors of pollution. For example, in discussing Rachel Carson's galvanizing work, *Silent Spring*, which analyzed how DDT and other pesticides were destroying birds and other wildlife, Lovelock asserted that DDT "will probably be more carefully and economically employed in future."[18] (Lovelock's Pollyannaish perspective is belied by the increased sale of DDT to the Third World after its use was banned in North America.)

Contending that chlorofluorocarbons (CFCs) are also "natural," Lovelock initially dismissed the fears of environmentalists that human-made CFCs resulting from aerosol cans, refrigerators, and air conditioners could have any sizable impact on ozone depletion. Methyl chloride, produced by the seas, he countered, breaks down ozone, as do CFCs, showing that too much ozone is as dangerous as is too little for Gaia.[19] Gaia, he suggests, has the situation under control. Revealingly, however, Lovelock in 1988 conceded that he may have been wrong to oppose those who wanted to legislate a reduction in CFCs, saying that he would now support such legislative restrictions in light of the disturbing evidence of ozone depletion.

Lovelock's dismissal of the important ozone depletion problem, a condition he brought to light through his own research, is a fascinating case study.[20] It highlights how scientists, enthralled by their own theories, can ignore data and minimize mammoth problems which belie their visions. It uncovers the limiting subjectivity of science and its all-too-human dimensions, and demonstrates how science itself is susceptible to social, political, and psychological pressures. Convinced that Gaia was robust and all-controlling, Lovelock had difficulty admitting that the pesky unfeathered bipeds of the human race could significantly injure it.[21]

Philosophical Responses to Gaia

During the 1980s, in addition to sparking debate within the Earth sciences, Gaia served as a galvanizing concept for New Age persons, globalists, and religious figures concerned about the environment. Dean James Morton of the (Episcopal) Cathedral of St. John of the Divine in New York commissioned a Missa Gaia by the eco-music group the Paul Winter Consort. Gaia Books in London, inspired by Lovelock's vision of the Earth as a single-living organism, prepared *Gaia: An Atlas of Planet Management*[22] and *The Gaia Peace Atlas: Survival into the Third Millennium*,[23] with contributions from scientists, church leaders, politicians, population experts, doctors, and environmentalists, all dedicated to preserving the Earth from decimation and arguing for the need to reharness human energy from war-making to Earth-keeping.[24] Books on Buddhism and Gaia, and myriad reflections on Gaia goddess imagery from an ecofeminist perspective, also emerged. These responses, which can be classified as pragmatic, philosophical, and theological, all discuss the role of the human within the Gaia framework, but with varying degrees of success.[25]

There are, at present, few sustained philosophical treatments of the Gaia theory. This is not surprising, given the theory's newness and its scientific focus. Perhaps the philosophic community is waiting for the scientific community's verdict before embarking on an enterprise whose subject matter may prove ephemeral. At any rate, William Irwin Thompson, a philosopher and cultural historian, has made Gaia something of a personal vocation in recent years. Formerly professor at MIT as well as at York University in Toronto, Thompson is presently director of the Lindisfarne Association, a relatively loose-knit concatenation of intellectuals dedicated to engendering what they term a "global culture." Believing that scientific theory is inevitably grounded in a grander philosophical and cultural narrative, Thompson sees in

Gaia a scientific yarn that could assist in stitching together a common planetary culture.[26]

For Thompson, our common understanding of "nature" is a fiction, a cultural construct influenced by Sierra Club calendars and the bucolic landscapes of 18th- and 19th-century British painters such as Paul Constable and Thomas Gainsborough. "Nature is the horizon of culture," Thompson avers, and depending on one's context, one's horizon will vary. Lovelock and Margulis help us to see this, he believes. Since in the Gaia framework, the division between animal, vegetable, and mineral is erased, all is "nature," wherever and whenever we look in the Gaian schema. The Gaia theory focuses on Earth processes, which offer insight into how culture operates and how we understand interrelationships among created realities.[27]

Although briefly involved in New Age currents, in the early eighties Thompson began looking for new avenues to a planetary consciousness and found in Gaia a promising vehicle. Believing that history is inevitably paradoxical, Thompson claims that humanity can never know fully what it is about; for the reasoning mind gains insight into one reality only by casting shadows upon another. The world is thus a structure of unconscious relations, and the relations of a global culture can only be the product of a process seemingly motored by avarice and fear. Gaia thus proffers a concrete cosmology within which these antinomies of history become comprehensible.

What is the role of the human in the Gaian framework? For Thompson, it appears to be simply to sit back and reconcile itself to a process in which we humans may be nothing more than a transitory phase. Rather than managing the planet, we are merely passengers on it, much like ants on a log, Thompson muses, drifting downstream, actively trying to steer that over which they have no control.[28] In promoting Lovelock and Margulis through his Lindisfarne Association, Thompson, it appears, is also promoting a limited role for the human in the Gaia process; he appears to be less involved in social action for the future sustainability of the planet than in "planetary consciousness-raising" through which we humans might reconcile ourselves to our microscopic function within the all-embracing Gaia.

Anthony Weston, with the department of philosophy at the State University of New York at Stony Brook, has a particular interest in environmental ethics, as well as the ethics of technology and medicine. He has explored what he terms the sundry "Forms of Gaian Ethics."[29] While claiming that Lovelock's Gaia theory is suggestive, Weston points out that what precisely it "suggests" is nebulous. He notes that Lovelock and Margulis emphasize Gaia's powers, rather than our human responsibilities, and that Lovelock has at times characterized ecologists as "misanthropes" and "Luddites."[30] Weston suggests, however, that there are at least two other ethical approaches one can adopt with regard to Gaia: one more commensurate with contemporary philosophical ethics, the other more akin to "deep ecology."

First, Weston postulates, for the sake of argument, that one could regard Gaia not simply as a living entity but as a person, thereby forcing, not a recasting of our ethical assumptions, but merely an expansion of our understanding of person to include other realities. In this manner, we might challenge, not the ethical centrality of persons, but the presupposition that only humans can be counted as persons.[31] While such an approach appeals to a long ethical history of the rights of persons, Weston finds it fulsomely anthropocentric in light of our current ecological situation, and also too facile a maneuver. For Weston, Gaia ultimately is not a person but a novel locus of values.[32]

Secondly, noting the correspondence between deep ecology and the Gaia theory, Weston comments that both view humans merely as just one species among many in the vast sweep of the Earth's processes, offering what deep ecologist Arne Naess calls a "total field" conception. In this understanding, we humans can only comprehend ourselves as elements of a much fuller and older life process. As such we sense the destruction of the Earth; we feel in our bowels, as it were, the destruction of the rain forest. Hence our visceral connection to Gaia helps us empathize and therefore resist the destruction of the planet.

Weston counters that such an approach presupposes a level of communication and identification among the Earth's species that even the Gaia theorists do not detect. The Gaia metaphor can be stretched too far to claim an intelligence for Gaia, an intelligence which simply may not exist.[33] Weston also argues that such an approach devalues non-animate matter, such as rocks and hills, and he worries about the environmental costs of such a devaluation. "Persons are not the only things that have value," he notes, "and neither is life itself."[34] For Weston, the answer lies not in substituting Gaia for another ethical framework, but in assimilating Gaia within the already existing variety of environmental values. Gaia doesn't necessarily have a single meaning or interpretation, but in its varied meanings, it could help point us toward the interrelationship of various value systems.

Theological Responses to Gaia

Douglas John Hall: Reintegrating Creation. In Amsterdam during May 1987, James Lovelock and Canadian Protestant theologian Douglas Hall, along with a handful of others, conferred for about a week to discuss the ecological crisis. Invited by the World Council of Churches as a follow-up to the call from Vancouver in 1983 to engage the churches in a commitment to "justice, peace, and the integrity of creation," the British scientist and the Canadian theologian emerged from their huddle with a discussion paper entitled "Reintegrating God's Creation." Intriguingly, Hall's paper does not deal with the Gaia theory directly. Rather, he discusses the nature of the term "integrity of creation" and the human role in it in the light of our destructive ecological habits.

As a Christian theologian, Hall professes that he cannot, as some deep ecologists do, support those who advocate a human retreat from intervention in the world. Rather, he proposes a contextual and strategic theology, one which walks the narrow path between what he terms "prometheanism" (a destructive glorification of human power) and passivity.[35]

Hall offers three roles for the Christian: steward (which he further develops in a book by the same title), priest, and poet. The steward enacts solidarity, accountability, and responsibility—all providing caring leadership. The priest represents God before the "creature" and represents the "creature" before God, acting as an empathetic and compassionate mediator in reintegrating a world broken by environmental despoliation. The poet, as rooted in the prophetic tradition of ancient Israel, celebrates the creaturely joys and visceral pain of being part of the created world, speaking not only for the human, but also for other creatures that inhabit the universe.[36] For Hall, then, the role of the human is central to an environmental theology. But, although he was metaphorically in dialogue with Gaia during his conversations with Lovelock, he does not use Gaia as an overarching paradigm. In fact, neither he nor Lovelock ever refers to it in their working paper.

Rosemary Radford Ruether: Gaia and God. By far the most substantial work by a Christian theologian on some of the implications of the Gaia theory, Ruether's *Gaia and God: An Ecofeminist Theology of Earth-Healing* vividly illustrates how the environmental crisis is forcing a major re-examination of the underpinnings of Western culture. From the thought of ancient Babylonian, Mesopotamian, Hebraic, Greco-Roman, early Christian, and Native American cultures, Ruether sifts for golden nuggets that might help us eschew ecological suicide. Undergirding Ruether's project is an examination of the underside of Western civilization's treatment of women and nature, showing how deeply embedded such destruction, domination, and deceit are in our culture.

While providing a helpful and terse overview of the Gaia theory, Ruether does not tease out its ethical and theological ramifications directly. She notes that it has become an instrument of ecofeminists who find in an Earth goddess a way of avoiding a pernicious male deity but sagely cautions against such an interchangeable approach to God.

Dedicated to eco-justice, Ruether is critical of militarism, sexism, consumerism, and systemic poverty and injustice, all of which constitute threats to organic life. Assuming that the Earth forms a living system and averring that we humans are an "inextricable part" of that system, she opposes the Western conception of nature that is both non-human and non-divine[37] and claims that our ethical standards should reflect the interdependency proposed by Gaia. Lynn Margulis and James Lovelock have given us a new vision of the Earth in which cooperation is as important as competition. "Human ethics should be a more refined and conscious version of the natural interdependency, mandating humans to imagine and feel the suffering of others, and to find ways in which interrelation becomes cooperative and mutually life-enhancing for both sides."[38] For Ruether, both the Gaia theory of Lovelock and Margulis and the new cosmology of cultural historian Thomas Berry and mathematician Brian Swimme counter the Cartesian mechanistic view of nature, and help dissolve traditional dualisms that have had such deleterious consequences for both women and nature.

In this well-researched, encyclopedic study, Ruether accepts the emerging scientific stories, such as Gaia and the universe story, and unpacks their ethical implications. Outlining the human agenda in light of such scientific insights, she rehearses ideas that others in the ecological movement have also advanced: bioregionalism, reduced population, organic farming, an end to militarism and destructive technologies, global economic justice, communities of solidarity and alternative lifestyles, and an ability to listen to nature (a chief feature of Thomas Berry's thought).[39] Somewhat surprisingly, however, she does not squarely address the theological questions posed by Gaia.

Thomas Berry: Gaia in a Cosmological Context. For Thomas Berry, a Passionist priest and "geologian," the wellsprings of the Gaia theory are part of a continuum through which a new sense of the sacredness of the cosmos is emanating from modern science. With his own work deeply influenced by contemporary physics and astronomy, as evidenced by his recent collaboration with mathematician Brian Swimme on *The Universe Story,* Berry argues that theories of relativity, quantum physics, the uncertainty principle of Heisenberg, the sense of a self-organizing universe, and the more recent chaos theories have gotten us beyond Cartesian mechanistic thinking and into an interrelated understanding of our world. Gaia is a part of these developments.

In his article "The Gaia Theory: Its Religious Implications," Berry claims that we need a Gaia theory, but we also need a cosmological context in which to place it. For Berry, the universe is the primary revelatory event: knowing and relating the story of the universe's unfolding, from the Big Bang or "primordial flaring forth" some 15 billion years ago to the present, become of primary religious significance. The human is now in the driver's seat of geological evolution, moving us out of the Cenozoic Era into either the "Technozoic" era, in which we continue to plunder the planet, or the "Ecozoic" era, in which we live within its functioning. For Berry, the choice is ours. Unlike Lovelock, Berry ascribes a momentous role to the human. Not only are we now the architects of evolutionary history, but we are also the beings in whom the universe becomes self-conscious and through whom it is able to reflect upon itself. Such a massive role for the human in the cosmos has caused some to critique Berry's thought for its potentially dangerous anthropocentrism.

In essence, Berry uses the Gaia theory as a springboard for his own reflections on the mystical dimensions of the cosmos. More often than not, his religious views are more connected to the views of animistic or shamanistic faiths than to Christian tradition. As several commentators have pointed out, Berry's cosmological vision is rarely related to Christian categories, and his universal story lacks a coherent plan of social action, a point made by Jon Sobrino, Paul Knitter, and Gregory Baum.

A Christian Political Theology of the Environment

The Gaia theory raises a host of questions for those wishing to engage in a political theology of the environment. Many of these questions revolve around the role of the human in the Gaian schema. Are we humans mere blips, a short-lived, destructive species with little lasting impact on the planet, as Margulis, Lovelock, and William Irwin Thompson propose? Should we assimilate Gaia into a pre-existing set of environmental values, reconciling ourselves to a pluriform ethical schema, as Anthony Weston suggests? Shall we take the cooperative model advanced by Gaia as a blueprint for an ethic of Earth-healing, as advanced by Rosemary Ruether? Are we called to be stewards, priests, and poets in light of the ecological crisis, as proffered by Douglas John Hall? Or are we the self-consciousness of the universe, as postulated by Thomas Berry?

Beyond these questions, however, are pressing social justice issues and the concerns of a political theology of the environment. Is Gaia useful for a Christian social justice perspective on environmental destruction? Does Gaia provide a suitable framework for articulating the role of the human within such a social justice perspective? From the perspective of social justice, the world is a political economy, a structure of power relationships in which there are "haves" and "have-nots." Can Gaia be understood as a political economy in which the poor nations, particularly of the South, bear the brunt of ecological destruction? A social justice perspective posits a preferential option for the poor. Is such an option viable within a Gaian framework? Lastly, a social justice perspective ascribes special responsibilities to persons and governments of Northern nations in effecting a just global community. Can Gaia sharpen our insight into North-South differences and help develop a model of action which takes into account these differences?

Gaia *is* helpful for a social justice perspective in several ways. As Lovelock himself comments, Gaia helps us to look at the world, not as a mechanistic Cartesian engine, but as an interrelated, vital, and cooperative enterprise in which interdependency rather than competition is the hallmark of life, revealing at the same time that the context in which human praxis is waged is also one of critical and unavoidable interconnectedness. Adding to the key insight of European political theology, Third World liberation theology, and feminist theology that a transformative theology must be contextual, Gaia forces us to expand our notion of context beyond social, economic, and political dimensions to include a critical planetary dimension.

Gaia has, however, serious limitations for a social justice perspective. It is ahistorical-agnostic in terms of human history. It lacks an analysis of existing power structures as well as historical patterns of inequality in which political praxis occurs. Moreover, it underestimates the destructive potency of the human species. By viewing humans as simply one life form among many, and a largely inessential one at that, Gaia woefully undervalues the human ability to destroy the life systems of the planet. Hence Gaia ultimately lacks a framework for critically assessing and challenging exploitative human activity.

Perhaps the ultimate value of Gaia lies in the fact that it prompts us to envisage our world in a novel, challenging, and inspirational way, as the burgeoning literature around it attests. The question as to whether or not the theory is "true" is, in the end, secondary to whether it helps us link justice and peace to the integrity of all creation. Gaia, I believe, can help us forge this still fragile but necessary nexus, as long as we remain aware of both its evocative power and its grave limitations.

Born Again: Liberation Theology

L iberation theology is dead. It hasn't had a new thought in years. So pronounced a distinguished Canadian theologian to me during a personal conversation several years ago. Fortunately, this professor was wrong.

At a recent meeting of the American Academy of Religion in San Diego, Calif., however, where more than 10,000 theologians and scholars of religion met to discuss their academic wares, liberation theology was anything but moribund.

A new book series, *Reclaiming Liberation Theology*, was launched there and several lively and well-attended sessions on new developments in the field were featured. The seminars also featured several young authors pursuing issues such as racism, aboriginal rights, sexism, and the "idolatry" of market capitalism—subjects that mark fresh directions for the movement.

Springing from the barrios of Latin America during the 1960s, liberation theology asserted that Christians could not be neutral in the face of social and economic injustice. It argued that the Church must adopt what the 1968 Latin American Bishops Conference termed a "preferential option for the poor."

At that time the Church had an often cozy and beneficial relationship with oppressive dictatorships and brutally unjust economic systems. It urged the church, in effect, to lay down its traditional teaspoons of charity and climb aboard the bulldozers of justice.

Not surprisingly, liberation theology stepped on a lot of political and ecclesial toes. One reason it became so controversial was that many priests openly sympathized with the oppressed and so became government targets, especially in Nicaragua, El Salvador and Guatemala.

During the height of El Salvador's civil war in the mid-1980s, for example, pamphlets reading "Be a patriot. Kill a priest" were widely distributed. Eighteen priests were assassinated during the conflict.

Many of its leading exponents, such as Archbishop Oscar Romero, were killed, and many of its leading theorists—Leonardo Boff and most recently Jon Sobrino—have been silenced or censured by the Vatican.

Cardinal Joseph Ratzinger, now Pope Benedict XVI, led the ecclesial crusade against liberation theology, penning a 1984 critique of its allegedly Marxist interpretation of the gospel.

Ivan Petrella's recent book, *The Future of Liberation Theology*, shows the continuing relevance of the movement as Latin nations strive for social justice and stronger democracies. According to Petrella, "Liberation theology is controversial because it wrests knowledge away from the wealthy and powerful. In doing so, it demands a shift in thinking about the world so radical that it's really nothing less than a conversion."

For example? "The UN Human Development Report once noted that it would take an additional yearly investment of $6 billion to assure basic education for everyone, while $8 billion is spent annually on cosmetics in the U.S. The report also noted that an additional $9 billion of investment would take care of clean water, while $11 billion a year is spent on ice cream in Europe," Petrella says.

"What does this data have to do with Christianity? Until liberation theology came along, nothing. And that's the point."

While many liberation theologians are dead, the concept clearly is not. And, in light of growing poverty and economic inequity both in Toronto and around the world, it seems it will remain germane for a long time to come.

Ecofeminism:
From Patriarchy to Mutuality

Racism, sexism, class exploitation, and ecological destruction are four interlocking pillars upon which the structure of patriarchy rests.

Sheila Collins, *A Different Heaven and Earth*

Ecofeminism, for several reasons, is a pivotal development for those fashioning a political theology of the environment.

First, ecofeminist theology, as espoused particularly by Rosemary Radford Ruether, has been at the vanguard of a religiously oriented social ecology, which attempts to delineate the connections among social, cultural, religious, economic, political, and ecological exploitation. Consequently, ecofeminism is built upon social analysis that scrutinizes interlocking dualisms perceived to be oppressive of both women and nature.

Second, ecofeminist theology has endeavored to locate a liberative role for the human amid such intersecting circles of exploitation. Through a critique of patriarchal dimensions of classical philosophy and the Judeo-Christian heritage, as well as Enlightenment traditions of the autonomous and objective self and the perception of nature as mechanistic and nonsacred, ecofeminists seek a transformed notion of the human that erases hierarchical, patriarchal dualisms undergirding patterns of dominance. For the theological ecofeminist, the encounter with the divine should lead to a human role marked neither by domi-nance nor by exploitation, but by mutuality.[1]

Third, as a theology of emancipation, ecofeminism adopts a self-critical and transformative stance. Its objective is not merely to understand ecologically and culturally pernicious structures but to transform them with sustained critique and sustainable alternatives.

What Is Ecofeminism?

While there are myriad approaches within ecofeminism, a com-mon insight is that in Eurocentric societies there is a forceful nexus between the manner in which women and that in which nature are viewed, specifically, with trepidation, resentment, and denigration.[2] Ecofeminists find within a Western patriarchal framework an unmis-takable "logic of domination" that extends to the nonhuman world.

Ethicist Karen Warren asserts that just as patriarchal culture fosters racism and sexism, it also engenders "naturism":

> Ecofeminists insist that the sort of logic of domination used to justify the domination of humans by gender, racial, ethnic, or class status is also used to justify the domination of nature. Because eliminating a logic of domination is part of a feminist critique—whether a critique of patriarchy, white supremacist culture, or imperialism—ecofeminists insist that naturism is properly viewed as an integral part of any feminist solidarity movement to end sexist oppression and the logic of domina-tion which conceptually grounds it.[3]

Interlocking Dualisms

In order to comprehend this logic of domination, ecofeminists study the interrelated dualisms of Western culture: male/female, mind/body, human/nonhuman, culture/nature, white/nonwhite, heaven/Earth, independence/interdependence, and so on.[4] Such dualisms, it is argued, reduce diversity into an either-or scenario.

Not only does this rigid separation undercut a mutuality that may exist between the two categories, but it also renders the second part of each dichotomy both inferior to and in the service of the first, ecofeminists argue. Hence, women serve men; nature serves culture; animals serve humans; nonwhites serve whites; and so forth.[5]

Ecofeminism has traced the dualisms that mark European patriarchal culture to (1) classical philosophy and the Judeo-Christian heritage (Rosemary Radford Ruether and E. Dodson Gray); (2) modern European mechanistic thought and Enlightenment focus on autonomy and objectivity (Carolyn Merchant and Vandana Shiva); and (3) the evisceration of Earth's sacredness in light of a transcendent "Sky God" (Charlene Spretnak, Starhawk, Sallie McFague).[6]

Historically, ecofeminists claim, women and the physical world have experienced similar exploitation under a structure of male supremacy. The interconnection of woman and nature has been reinforced by the personification of nature as female, as seen in the terms "Mother Nature" and "Mother Earth" and the tradition (now jettisoned) of giving hurricanes female names. While some of these identifications have nurturing intimations, other terms reveal an exploitative side to such identification, such as "virgin land" or "virgin stands of timber"—places yet to be cultivated by males. Moreover, the term "raping the land" derives from the violent sexual assault of women.[7]

Regarding religions, ecofeminists observe that the prevailing patriarchy of Western civilization is grounded in a spirituality that attempts to transcend nature and the body—particularly the female body. Such a patriarchal spirituality connects body, women, and nature and then preaches transcendence of the body and nature, thus sanctifying oppression.[8] Consequently, ecofeminists attempt to foster ideas and practices that perceive both nature and the body as sacred and spiritually revelatory.[9]

Rosemary Radford Ruether tersely defines the theological aspects of ecofeminism:

> The *theology* of ecofeminism brings feminist theology into dialogue with a culturally based critique of the ecological crisis. Patriarchal ideology perceives the earth or nature as a female or as a feminine reality. As such, nature is considered to be

inferior to men. As a material being having no spirit, no life in and of itself, nature is only a tool to be exploited by men. The cultural roots of the ecological crisis can be found in this common perception of both women and nature as realities without spirit and tools to be exploited by dominant males.[10]

A New Wave of Analysis

Ecofeminist analysis objects to separating culture into separate spheres—for example, politics from spirituality, human from nonhuman nature—seeing such divides as patriarchal dualisms. And yet it critiques any syncretisms that eschew political analysis. As Carol Adams writes in *Ecofeminism and the Sacred*:

> We are deeply engaged with political and economic struggles, as well as with the challenge to articulate ecofeminist theory. This is why ecofeminism has been called the third wave of feminism. Ecofeminism may have grown out of earlier feminist theory, but it revises this theory by its position that an environmental perspective is necessary for feminism. In demonstrating how a patriarchal culture "naturalizes" the domination of nature, of women, and of different races, this third wave of feminism can play a significant part in linking feminism with other social movements.[11]

In response to claims that ecofeminism is widely diffuse, Adams claims that ecofeminist analysis is not characterized by unity of thought, but by solidarity. Moreover, this solidarity is joined by interrelationship, transformation, and embodiment—the common threads of ecofeminist spirituality.[12]

In the following sections, we will review the work of three ecofeminists—Rosemary Radford Ruether, Sallie McFague, and Vandana Shiva—noting both points of conflict and convergence in their approaches to ecofeminism, their understanding of nature, and the role of the human.

Rosemary Radford Ruether:
Appealing to the Prophetic Tradition

> *Women must see that there can be no liberation for them and no solution to the ecological crisis within a society whose fundamental model of relationships continues to be one of domination. They must unite the demands of the women's movement with those of the ecological movement to envision a radical reshaping of the basic socioeconomic relations and the underlying values of this society.*

Rosemary Radford Ruether, *New Woman/New Earth*

Rosemary Radford Ruether[13] was among the first to show the connection between female and natural oppression.[14] Ever since the publication of Ruether's *New Woman/New Earth*, analysis of the twin oppression of nature and women has been a centerpiece of ecofeminist writings. As Ruether comments:

> Since women in Western culture have been traditionally identified with nature, and nature, in turn, has been seen as an object of domination by man (males), it would seem almost a truism that the mentality that regarded the natural environment as an object of domination drew upon imagery and attitudes based on male domination.[15]

Culture Critique

Ruether's power as a theologian lies largely in her ability to cut wide swaths through cultural patterns of oppression and structure them in a consistent narrative. Because of her training in the social and intellectual history of Christianity, her work reveals a historical methodology. This methodology has been used over the years to probe a variety of social issues: racism, religious prejudice, anti-Semitism, sexism, class conflict, colonialism, militarism, and ecological despoliation. In delineating the myriad ideological patterns in the Christian legacy that have condoned violence and subjugation, Ruether concludes that they all stem from a single root. In each of these ideologies, the prevailing social hierarchy and power relationships are affirmed and sanctified

by the claim that they emerge from the order of creation and are or-
dained by divine will.[16]

For Ruether, such a schema is most vividly manifest in sexism.
The superiority of men over women is perceived as a reflection of
the superiority of God, cast as male, over creation and the church,
envisioned as female. This pattern of domination dovetails with a
spirit-matter dichotomy. Men are seen as having superior rationality
and thus are more suited to places of power. Women, allegedly bereft
of these qualities, must by nature take a back seat to male authority.[17]

For Ruether, the basic dualisms—alienation of the mind from
the body, separation of the subjective self from the objective world,
the inferiority of nature to spirit—all have their provenance in the
apocalyptic-Platonic roots of classical Christianity.[18] Moreover, racism, classism, and human suppression of nonhuman nature are also
modeled after this mind-over-body duality.

Redemptive Lineaments of Our Cultural Heritage

Despite her thoroughgoing critique of the Platonic and Judeo-
Christian patriarchal heritage, Ruether does uncover within the classical patriarchal legacy elements of liberation, in which injustice is
assailed, and love and solidarity among persons and with the Earth are
proclaimed. (Such "treasures" are perhaps what keeps Ruether working
within the Judeo-Christian religion, rather than outside of it, where
other onetime Christian feminists have chosen to toil.)

For Ruether, the Psalms and the prophetic, covenantal tradition of
the Hebrew Scriptures and the New Testament hold particular power
for an ecofeminist perspective, as does the Judeo-Christian sacramental
tradition.[19] The prophetic tradition, according to Ruether, engenders
a move in the social location of religion. Rather than speaking for
the privileged and powerful, the prophetic tradition speaks on behalf
of the poor and marginalized within society. The prophets decry the
injustices of the ruling political, economic, and social powers, calling
them to account for their subversion of the biblical call for justice and
compassion. God punishes in order to foster repentance, and through
repentance the society will be restored to the authentic divine wish

for humans to live justly with one another and harmoniously with nonhuman nature.[20]

The Hebrew prophetic tradition, Ruether argues, is concerned primarily with the crushing of the poor by the rich and is against the imperial regimes of the Near East that subjugated the tribes of Israel. The agricultural heritage of the Hebrew people, moreover, yields an implicit ecological theology. Human injustice and sin breach the covenant with Yahweh, resulting in divine wrath and natural destruction. However, the covenantal promise intimates the recrudescence of peace and fertility when justice and righteousness in the society are restored.

According to Ruether, the New Testament expands this critical vision to a catholic redemptive community unfettered by an ethnic identification of those who achieve "God's smile" of election. She finds particular promise in the Pauline understanding of a dissolution of difference in the umbrella of Christ, where subordinate relations between Jew and Greek, male and female, slave and master are transformed.[21]

Role of Nature

Given her account on ecojustice, it is not surprising that Ruether perceives nature largely shaped by the human, rather than as largely distinct from unfeathered bipeds. For her, nonhuman nature is not an objective reality to which we can simply "return." Rather, it is a product of both evolutionary and human emergence. Nowhere on Earth is there such a thing as "pristine nature," untouched by human hands. Everywhere, the smudge of human pollution is manifest, even if only in trace air, soil, and air contaminants. In this sense, Ruether sees nature as "fallen," owing not to any intrinsic evil but to misguided human advancement.[22] Thus, renewing our relationship with nature is a process of re-creating something novel, not returning to a previous unvitiated state.[23] Here, the project takes on the dimension of a new vision:

> Nature will never be the same as it would have been without human intervention. Although we need to remake the earth in a way that converts our minds to nature's logic of ecological harmony, this will necessarily be a new synthesis, a new creation

in which human nature and nonhuman nature become friends in the creating of a livable and sustainable cosmos.[24]

A Gaian Guide

Ruether also engages contemporary scientific theory in her feminist writings, most notably, the Gaia theory. In *Gaia and God,* she provides a helpful and terse overview of the scientific Gaia theory—first espoused by British atmospheric scientist James Lovelock—that, as sketched earlier, claims that Earth is a self-regulating, living organism. Speaking of the religious reverberations of Gaia, a term that also denotes the ancient Greek goddess of the Earth, Ruether notes that it had become an instrument of ecofeminists who see an Earth goddess as a way of avoiding a pernicious male deity. She sagely cautions against, however, such an interchangeable approach to God:

> The term Gaia has caught on among those seeking a new ecological spirituality as a religious vision. Gaia is seen as a personified being, an immanent divinity. Some see the Jewish and Christian male monotheistic God as a hostile concept that rationalizes alienation from and neglect of the earth. Gaia should replace God as our focus of worship. I agree with much of this critique, yet I believe that merely replacing a male transcendent deity with an immanent female one is an insufficient answer to the "god-problem."[25]

Ruether assumes that Earth forms a living system, thereby accepting a key premise of the Gaia theory, and stresses that we humans are an "inextricable part" of that system. She opposes a Western concept of nature as both nonhuman and nondivine and claims that our ethical standards should reflect Gaia's interdependency. Lynn Margulis and James Lovelock, she notes, have given us a new vision of Earth through Gaia, in which cooperation is as important as competition. "Human ethics should be a more refined and conscious version of the natural interdependency, mandating humans to imagine and feel the suffering of others, and to find ways in which interrelation becomes cooperative and mutually life-enhancing for both sides."[26] For Ruether, both the Gaia theory of Lovelock and microbiologist Lynn Margulis and the new cosmology of cultural historian Thomas Berry and mathematician Brian Swimme counter the Cartesian mechanistic view of nature and help dissolve traditional dualisms that have had such a deleterious legacy for both women and nature.

Ruether, it seems, embraces much of the emerging scientific stories such as Gaia and the universe story, unpacking, however, more of their ethical than their theological implications. In outlining the human agenda in light of such scientific insights, Ruether rehearses the ideas that others in the ecological movement have also advanced: bioregionalism, reduced populations, organic farming, an end to militarism and destructive technologies, global economic justice, communities of solidarity and alternative lifestyles, and an ability to listen to nature (a chief feature of Thomas Berry's thought).[27] Somewhat surprisingly, however, the theological questions posed by Gaia are not directly addressed.

In Ruether's earlier writings, the role of the human within this matrix is one of a "gardener" who works with the forces of nature to fructify rather than exploit. This seems slightly superseded, however, as she ponders the human role in the context of Gaia, where we are to learn to cooperate among ourselves in keeping with the workings of the living organism, Gaia.

A New Humanity

Reflecting the thought of Latin American liberation theologians, Ruether proposes that the role of the human, ultimately, is to create a "new humanity" within a "new society," one in which cooperation, rather than domination, is the core principle and sex-stereotyping and culturally nurtured oppression would be curtailed. Ruether elucidates this "new society":

> The center of such a new society would have to be not just the appropriate new social form, but a new social vision, a new soul that would inspire the whole. Society would have to be transfigured by the glimpse of a new type of social personality, a "new humanity" appropriate to a "new earth."[28]

Such a society, she muses, no longer directed toward destroying the Earth, might have greater time for contemplation, leading not to a quarantined understanding of the self but to one that saw the self in affirmation of others and in solidarity with others, the Earth, "and the thou with whom I am in a state of reciprocal interdependence."[29]

Third World Colloquy

Since the early 1990s, Ruether has fostered a dialogue between First World ecofeminists and Third World women who draw links between oppression of land and of women.[30] In so doing, Ruether issues a challenge to privileged white North American ecofeminists to move beyond psycho-spiritual understandings of nature, with their "exultant experiences of the rising moon and seasonal wonders," to embrace the realities of the plurality of the world's women, who are poor and exploited in a fearsome manner. Such psycho-spiritual reconnection with nature can become a "recreational self-indulgence," she argues, if the connection with the overconsumption and waste is not emphasized. Such self-indulgence will occur, she warns in *Women Healing Earth: Third World Women on Ecology, Feminism, and Religion,*

> if the healing of our bodies and our imaginations as Euro-Americans is not connected concretely with the following realities: ... the top 20 percent of the world's human population enjoys 82 percent of the wealth while the other 80 percent scrapes along with 18 percent; and the poorest 20 percent of the world's people, over a *billion* people—disproportionately women and children—starve and die from early poisoned waters, soil, and air.[31]

Here, Ruether manifests once again her liberationist provenance as a theologian. Solidarity and a preferential inclination toward the poor, in this case, poor women and children, remain for her the starting points of any viable and transformative theological stance.

Sallie McFague: The Quest for Embodiment Transforming Divine and Human Models

Most Westerners, quite unselfconsciously, believe in the sacredness of every individual human being (while scarcely

protesting the extinction of all the members of other species);
believe males to be "naturally" superior to females; find human
fulfillment (however one defines it) more important than the
well-being of the planet; and picture God as a distant, almighty
superperson ... Christianity is surely not alone responsible for
this worldview, but to the extent that it has contributed to and
supported it, the deconstruction of some of its major metaphors
and the construction of others is in order.

Sallie McFague, *"A Square in the Quilt"*

Like Rosemary Radford Ruether, Sallie McFague[32] believes that the role of the theologian is not merely description, formulation, or analysis but advocacy and transformation. For her, the theological enterprise must be characterized not by "soloists" striving to pen the monumental, all-encompassing systematic theology but rather by "advocates" of a sustainable future, working collegially and respecting differences among their counterparts.[33] Her particular contribution to the ecofeminist perspective, or, as she claims, her "piece of the quilt," is to invite Christian theology to consider new models and metaphors for God.

In *Models of God: Theology for an Ecological, Nuclear Age,*[34] McFague, who has a background in literature, launches an evocative critique of the monarchical model of God that has for so long dominated Christian art, prayer, and worship. Building upon feminist analysis, McFague argues that the monarchical model is deeply anthropocentric, marked by dualistic hierarchies. While the image of God as king may not directly be responsible for hierarchical dualism, it has reinforced, she claims, such splits as "male/female, spirit/nature, human/nonhuman, Christian/non-Christian, rich/poor, white/colored, and so forth."[35]

Moreover, in the monarchical model, she continues, God is removed from the world, distant from "his subjects," and engaged only with the human rather than the nonhuman world. In addition, he is far above his subjects, for royalty is "untouchable." Whatever one does for the world is insignificant in this image, "for its ruler does not inhabit it as his primary residence, and his subjects are well advised not to become enamored of it either."[36] Ultimately, the preservation of the Earth within the kingly model is God's problem, not ours. (Significantly, McFague does not allude to the ancient Christian councils, which depict God not as monarch but as Triune, "over and above" as Father and "in and through" as Spirit.)

Searching for Ecological Models of God

God as Mother, Lover, Friend

In place of the monarch, McFague initially proposes the models of God as Mother, lover, and friend.[37] Such models, which have biblical lineage, can help Christianity, McFague believes, eschew some of the patriarchal dualisms and domineering aspects of the monarchical model and open up new ways to be in solidarity not only with other persons but with nonhuman nature as well.[38]

Describing her theology as "heuristic," McFague claims that theology's traditional quest for truth has often led it to suppress all imaginative metaphors. Because no language about God is sufficient, she asserts, novel metaphors are not per se less sufficient than previous ones. In this sense, all share a similar status, and no putative authority can declare that some images refer directly to God while others do not, because, ultimately, none do. Thus, the criteria for choosing some images over others transcends "authority," however defined.[39]

The Universe or World as God's Body

McFague also elucidates the metaphor of the world as God's body,[40] building upon an image proposed by process philosopher Charles Hartshorne.[41] McFague believes that only an embodied metaphor of God can escape the dualistic, patriarchal images of the divine that have helped nurture both the oppression of women and the destruction of nature. For her, such an organic model is the cornerstone of a theology of nature that must (1) reflect contemporary scientific understandings of the universe, or what McFague calls "the common creation story"; (2) perceive humans as deeply interrelated with all other forms of life; (3) focus more on creation than redemption; and (4) stress the nexus between ecological issues and justice and peace issues, furthering the connection of "justice, peace, and the integrity of creation" proposed by the World Council of Churches.[42]

The springboard for all of this, for McFague, is the "common creation story" being told by what she calls "postmodern" science. Seeking a "loose fit" between science and theology, McFague claims that the common creation story is the one creation narrative that all humans, nonhumans, indeed, "everything that is," has in common. It is connected with the big bang theory of the universe's beginnings some 13 billion years ago. Because the story is "common" (i.e., incorporates all that is), it is different from sundry religious cosmologies; however, while being inclusive, it also maintains radical diversity and individuality.[43]

In keeping with this story, McFague suggests that God is the embodied spirit of the cosmos. This embodiment is a model that entails both personal and organic images and, she argues, is commensurate with interpretation by both the Christian faith and contemporary science, which speaks of a common origin and kinship of all that exists. This model, for McFague, emphasizes our bodiliness and raises the notion of responsibility toward all bodies that are interrelated and mutually dependent.[44]

Although other Christian ecological thinkers, such as Thomas Berry (discussed above), also appeal to the common creation story emerging in science, McFague is distinctive in her attempt to embrace a social justice perspective in its adoption. Although not engaged in the type of social and cultural analysis that is the hallmark of Ruether's work, McFague reveals a deep sensitivity to liberation theology and the plight of marginalized and impoverished persons, especially women.

She notes that ecological deterioration hits those who are least responsible for it: the inhabitants of the "under-consuming" nations of the Third World. As she illustratively writes in *The Body of God*:

> To put the matter in a nutshell, a Third-World woman of color (as well as her First-World sister in the ghettoes of major cities) is the most impacted person on the planet. Her greatest

ecological sin is probably ravaging denuded forests to gather firewood to cook her family's dinner. The most responsible person is a First-World, usually white, usually male, entrepreneur involved in a high-energy, high-profit business. His (her) greatest ecological discomfort is probably having to suffer through a record-breaking hot weekend when the air conditioner broke down and no repair person would come to fix it until Monday. As more of the earth becomes desert, water scarcer, air more polluted, food less plentiful, the lines between the "haves" and the "have nots" will become even more sharply drawn. Justice for the oppressed will recede from view when resources become scarce. If the human population doubles in forty or fifty years, as appears likely, and the pressure on the planet for the basics of existence intensifies, those with power will do what is necessary to insure their own piece of the disappearing pie.[45]

Poor People and an Impoverished Planet

In an evocative discussion, McFague implies that nature is the "new poor" and attempts to develop a Christology from her personal/organic model that embraces this new poor. Nature is oppressed as are humans, though here McFague is speaking not simply of women but of all who are oppressed in a patriarchal consumer-driven culture. As she explains:

> Nature as the new poor does not mean that we should sentimentalize nature or slip into such absurdities as speaking of "oppressed" mosquitoes or rocks. Rather, nature as the new poor means that we have made nature poor. It is a comment not about the workings of natural selection but of human sin.[46]

In keeping with her focus on human sinfulness and responsibility regarding environmental destruction, McFague says the emergence of impoverished nature is a "cold, hard" reality of human transgression. We have, she asserts, ruptured the integrity of creation through overpopulation and consumption, through our instrumentalist approach to nature and to certain disenfranchised peoples, and by our unwillingness to respect the intrinsic and divine value of every aspect of creation. Seeing a nexus between the oppression of poor people and the subjugation of nature, McFague writes:

> This perspective claims that in the twentieth century on our planet, human beings have caused nature to be the new poor in the same way that a small elite of the human population has created and continues to create the old poor—through a gross imbalance of the have and have-nots. Those "other" people (the old poor) and nature (the new poor) are, in both cases, there "for our use."[47]

Role of the Human

What is the role of the human within this organic model of God? For one thing, McFague avers, ecology must become a primary vocation rather than a hobby or avocation. An ecological perspective, one that includes a notion of solidarity with both poor persons and destitute nature, must not be ancillary to the theological enterprise, but central.

Moreover, humans must see themselves not as lords and masters over creation but as products of creation, as derived from nature. In addition, humans have to learn to see themselves not as the "goal of creation" but rather as citizens of the Earth (a concept borrowed from Aldo Leopold) and "caretakers of the planet." (This in some way reflects Rosemary Radford Ruether's understanding of humans as gardeners.) McFague maintains that, as caretakers, we must see our interrelationship with all matter; we must serve as guardians given our special destructive patterns; and we must acknowledge our responsibility to fulfill the divine plan for life to continue:

> We have become, like it or not, the guardians and caretakers of our tiny planet. In a universe characterized by complex individuality beyond our comprehension, our peculiar form of individuality and interdependence has developed into a special role for us. We are the responsible ones, responsible for all the rest upon which we are so profoundly dependent.[48]

> We must learn to live within the rules of our *oikos*, our household, from which the word ecology derives, and act in partnership with God to see that life flourishes.[49]

While compelling, this depiction of the human as caretaker reflects the notion of stewardship held up by many theologians as the proper role of the human in light of the environmental crisis. While such a stance is welcome and represents a quantum leap from the modern understanding of humanity as plunderer of nature, one wonders whether it still maintains too much of a managerial flavor to be perduringly helpful. The radical interrelationship that McFague points to in the new common creation story suggests something far more intimate, something far more mutually constitutive in terms of the human relationship to nature. While the Gaia theorists unfortunately belittle the role of the human somewhat in effecting changes in nature (as seen in a previous chapter), they do indicate a crucial point—that we may not be more than "middle" or "upper-middle" management when it comes to running the planet.

As a Christian, McFague sees a compatibility between Jesus' role and our role in light of the environmental crisis. Through Jesus' life and passion, we see a twin response to the solidarity to which we are called—liberation and suffering. We are called to help liberate exploited persons and nature from human greed and sinfulness, while at the same time being asked to suffer for our solidarity, a reality that, as McFague points out, belies any naïve or sentimental understandings about communing with nature or quick results in achieving sustainability:

> Given human sin, the possibility for solidarity with the vulnerable to triumph or even make a significant difference is highly questionable, as anyone knows who has worked on any justice or ecological issue. Add to human sin the vagaries of natural evil, and one must accept the inevitability of intense and massive suffering.[50]

As the heinous assassination of Chico Mendes—a Brazilian rubber-tapper union leader struggling to preserve jobs and the rainforest—indicates, such solidarity with the "new poor" may well be met with the same type of violence that solidarity with the human indigent has elicited in the past. If it is true that the same forces who oppress poor persons also oppress nature, then the list of martyrs in Latin America and elsewhere in the Third World may well soon swell with the names of those who express solidarity both with the poor and with the Earth.

Vandana Shiva: From "Monoculture" to Diversity

Patriarchal Development and the Dual Assault on Women and Nature in the Third World

> We perceive development as a patriarchal project because it has emerged from centers of Western capitalist patriarchy, and it reproduces these patriarchal structures within the family, in community and throughout the fabric of Third World societies. Patriarchal prejudice colors the structures of knowledge as well as the structures of production and work that shape and are in turn shaped by "development" activity. Women's knowledge and work as integrally linked to nature are marginalized or displaced, and in their place are introduced patterns of thought and patterns of work that devalue the worth of women's knowledge and women's activities. This fragments both nature and society.
>
> Vandana Shiva, "Let Us Survive"

Though a physicist rather than a theologian, Vandana Shiva is one of the foremost ecofeminist writers of the South, and her work has great import for ecofeminist theology. Her insights concerning the twin oppression of nature and women within the process of "development" have resonance throughout so-called underdeveloped nations and, increasingly, throughout the North as well.[51]

Like Ruether and McFague, Shiva assails patriarchy as a prime adversary in the ecofeminist struggle. Yet, unlike her First World counterparts, she perceives patriarchy as having two distinct and parlous prongs: Western development schemes, which spawn a new colonialism, and modern science, which is destructive both of nature and of women's sustainable approaches to the Earth. From Shiva's vantage, "capitalist patriarchy has substituted the sacredness of life with the sacredness of science and development."[52]

This overarching patriarchy, in Shiva's view, forms a "monoculture," which destroys localized knowledge systems, such as that of women farmers and indigenous cultures, as well as diversified economies. In so doing, it replaces such knowledge systems with a top-down, First World, modern growth approach to economic and cultural development. This approach is epitomized for Shiva in World Bank policies, such as Structural Adjustment Programs (SAPs), which, in return for loans, compel Third World nations to open themselves to foreign investment; remove price subsidies of basic food stuffs such as milk, bread, and flour; convert agriculture from diversified, domestically consumed products to cash-export products; and generally remove local governments from decision-making processes in their own economies.[53] (In the words of U.S. consumer advocate Ralph Nader, such programs, linked to "free-trade" arrangements, make the world "safe *from* democracy.")

The "myth" of such a monoculture, Shiva argues, is that it is more productive than a diversified culture, whereas in actuality, it merely "controls more."[54] It has more to do with power than with production. In a striking parallel, Shiva notes that just as there was a disappearance of dissidents in the 1970s in Argentina under a brutal dictatorship, so now there is a disappearance of local knowledge systems throughout the Third World under the tyranny of the market economy, which brooks no dissent.[55]

Western Development: Depleting People and Nature

Grounded in numerous case studies of development projects in India and Sri Lanka, Shiva's penetrating analysis, reflecting while transcending the work of social theorists Andre Gunder Frank, Immanuel Wallerstein, Fernando H. Cardoso, and Enzo Faletto, argues that development is actually a form of neocolonialism. Rather than improving living conditions of those in the developing world, it has actually increased their poverty. Moreover, it hits women particularly hard, for their work, along with nature's productive capabilities, is both devalued and rendered "invisible." Subsistence economies, those working sustainably with the land and maintained by women, become ciphers in the developmentalist schema:

The displacement of women from productive activity by the expansion of development was rooted largely in the manner in which development projects appropriated or destroyed the natural resource base for the production of sustenance and survival. It destroyed women's productivity both by removing land, water and forests from their management and control, as well as through the ecological destruction of soil, water and vegetation systems so that nature's productivity and renewability were impaired. While gender subordination and patriarchy are the oldest of oppressions, they have taken on new and more violent forms through the project of development.[56]

Shiva perceives development as patriarchal because it rises from the centers of Western capitalist patriarchy and replicates patriarchal patterns within the families and communities of Third World societies. Women's knowledge and labor, she contends, are connected to nature, and as they are replaced by patriarchal, top-down modes of thought and work, both women and nature are fragmented.[57]

Today, she asserts, women and the natural environment of the Third World are both striving for emancipation from "development" just as, in years past, they vied for liberation from colonialism.[58] In essence, they are struggling to extricate themselves from what Shiva terms "maldevelopment," a form of development bereft of ecological principles, of an ethos of conservation, and of respect for women's skills and knowledge. In their stead, large-scale development projects, such as hydro-electric dams, are projected, which are geared more to help local elites than the majority of a nation's population, who are often displaced by such modern development projects.[59]

Reflecting much of the critique of development lodged by Gustavo Gutierrez and other liberation theologians during the late 1960s and early 1970s, Shiva takes the critique one step further, showing how development destroys nature as well as peoples and cultures. Concerning the developmentalist agenda, she writes:

The assumptions are evident: nature is unproductive; organic agriculture based on nature's cycles of renewability spells poverty; women and tribal and peasant societies embedded in nature are similarly unproductive, not because it has been demonstrated that in cooperation they produce *less* goods and services for needs, but because it is assumed the "production" takes place only when mediated by technologies for commodity production, even when such technologies destroy life.[60]

Hence, in this view, a clean, flowing river is not productive until it is severed by dams; women using the river to supply water to their families and communities are not involved in productive labor (male engineers, however, involved in water management and large-scale hydroelectric projects are doing productive work); forests are not productive until they are "developed" into a single crop plantation for export to help finance the foreign debt.[61]

Like economist Herman Daly and process theologian John B. Cobb Jr., Shiva is critical of economic measurements based on gross national product (GNP) or gross domestic product (GDP) standards. Such scales have no cost-accounting for the destruction of nature, failing to take into consideration the "gross *natural* product." Shiva trenchantly observes that indigenous peoples, indeed any peoples who do not participate wholeheartedly in the market economy, are immediately perceived as poor by those adopting a First World, developmental perspective. If they eat grains they have grown themselves, live in homes they have built, and wear locally designed and handmade garments from indigenous fiber, they are seen as impoverished. Subsistence and sustainability are perceived as misery.[62]

Critique of Modern Science

Just as a modern cash economy approach conflates indigenous economies with misery, so does modern science, according to Shiva, relegate indigenous knowledge and proximity to the land as primitive and inferior. Modern science, she observes, had its birth with Sir Francis Bacon (1561 – 1626) and helped advance male, middle-class entrepreneurs primarily. It was rooted in a quest for dominance and control over nature, and it disdained both women's skills and natural systems. In this sense, she argues, the modern scientific method has never been value-neutral but rather has always been male-oriented; the ideologies of modern science and gender were mutually reinforcing.[63]

For Shiva, modern science has achieved an almost unquestioned epistemological orthodoxy. Given its privileged position, and promoted by powerful First World nations, modern science attempts to supply technological nostrums for social and political problems that it cannot resolve, while simultaneously eschewing responsibility for the problems it itself creates.[64] As Shiva observes in *Monocultures of the Mind*, though modern Western knowledge has a particular relationship to power, it has projected itself as somehow transcending culture and politics and existing in the ethereal realm of "pure truth":

> Its [modern Western science's] relationship with the project of economic development has been invisible; and therefore it has become a more effective legitimizer for the homogenization of the world and the erosion of its ecological and cultural richness. The tyranny and hierarchy privileges that are part of the development drive are also part of the globalizing knowledge in which the development paradigm is rooted and from which it derives its rationalization and legitimization. The power by which the dominant knowledge system has subjugated all others makes it exclusive and undemocratic.[65]

The Virulence of the Green Revolution

Modern science reached much of the Third World in a direct way with the Green Revolution of the 1960s and 1970s. Envisioned as a technological and political agenda for peace and a way to eliminate hunger, the Green Revolution, Shiva argues, left much of the Third World more destitute and dependent—and ecologically ravaged—than before. She examines Punjab, the breadbasket of India, as a case study of such devastation. The promises of a quick technological corrective and of unprecedented output eclipsed, she argues, a serious quest for an alternative agricultural strategy. For her, such an alternative approach would be based on an acknowledgment of the environmental wisdom of peasant economies. Moreover, it would be rooted in a democratic, sustainable agriculture congruent with the village-oriented, autochthonous economic traditions of Mohandas Gandhi, an advocate of cottage-based industries. Shiva records the diminishment of genetic diversity and soil arability as a result of the chemical-intensive approach to agriculture in Punjab and suggests that the Green Revolution also helped foster the severe social and political strife experienced by the region in the 1980s.[66]

The Green Revolution eliminates diversity—it becomes a mono-culture that squelches or critiques as "primitive" alternative, sustainable, local approaches to agriculture.[67] A leitmotif of Shiva's diatribe against modern science, as it is enfleshed in the Green Revolution, is the supplanting of social, economic, and ecological diversity for social, economic, and ecological monocultures—the latter of which are vigorously promoted by First World nations, international lending agencies such as the IMF and World Bank, as well as global corporations.

A Baleful Biotechnology

Another perturbing outgrowth of modern science for Shiva is the new biotechnologies, which "tamper with the very fabric of life." While noting that biotechnology has existed in some form for centuries, Shiva explains that these new biotechnologies pose novel social, ecological, and economic threats.

Genetic engineering, for example, allows the transference of genes from one organism to another. Shiva argues that this innovation has the capacity to turn genes into a worldwide resource that can be utilized to mold new life-forms. While noting the positive benefits such biotechnologies have already shown in agriculture, forestry, chemicals, drugs, and foods, Shiva is deeply aware of the potential dangers of these breakthroughs.

First, though developed by small firms and universities, these new technologies are almost entirely controlled by transnational corporations, whose concern for profits sometimes outstrips caution in the use of these new "resources."

Second, citing a statement by scientists working on recombinant DNA molecules, Shiva avers that these new life-forms often pose serious and unpredictable biohazards, such as the possibility of artificial DNA molecules being introduced to *E. coli* bacteria, which could then exchange information with other types of bacteria, leading to their wide dissemination among human, bacterial, plant, or animal populations with unpredictable results.[68]

Moreover, Shiva punctures the myth that these new biotechnologies are ecologically benign and will lead to "chemically free agriculture." Building on the work of J. R. Kloppenburg and others,[69] Shiva notes that a number of principal agrochemical companies are bioengineering plants that are resistant to their herbicides, in hopes that they will be able to continue to sell their pesticides, while also peddling the seeds that can withstand them. For them, it's a win/win situation. For the Third World farmer, however, the situation is different: "For the Third World farmer his strategy for employing more toxic chemicals on pesticide and herbicide resistant varieties is suicidal, in a lethal sense. Thousands of people die annually as a result of pesticide poisoning."[70] Shiva advocates a Third World ban on the influx of herbicide-and pesticide-resistant crops owing to their health and ecological effects, as well as their economic and social impact, which includes labor disruption and the upsurge of capital-intensive farming.[71]

> Like Green Revolution technologies, biotechnology in agricul-
> ture can become an instrument for dispossessing the farmer
> of seed as a means of production. The relocation of seed pro-
> duction from the farm to the corporate laboratory relocates
> power and value between the North and South; and between
> corporations and farmers. It is estimated that the elimination
> of home grown seed would dramatically increase the farmers'
> dependence on biotech industries by about $6000 million US
> annually.[72]

Women and Ecological Movements

For Shiva, perceiving the connection between women and nature is not novel; what is new is realizing that women and nature are joined in a creative and life-sustaining way, as Third World women demonstrate. In contradistinction to many First World feminists, including Ruether and McFague to a certain extent, Shiva argues that Third World women are not primarily victims but leaders of a new social paradigm in relating to nature. Thus, Shiva labels her work a "post-victimology" enterprise. From her viewpoint, women's movements and ecological movements are the same—both are countervailing trends in light of patriarchal maldevelopment. Women involved in ecological movements seek to liberate themselves from oppression and nature from exploitation.[73] (Unfortunately, Shiva does not probe the involvement of women in the destruction and maintenance of patriarchy, nor does she discuss the role of women in the decimation of nature.)

Two of the women's movements Shiva points to are the Chipko and Appiko movements, indigenous, women-based initiatives to save forests and farmlands through "tree-hugging," timber-blockades, demonstrations, and other nonviolent measures. These protests have met with much success in India, and Shiva has served with them as participant and reflector. According to Shiva, these movements have gradually evolved from being based in conflicts over resources to clashes over modern scientific and instrumental approaches to nature—approaches that do not see the intrinsic value of the forest, its innate importance for rural agriculture, and the value and dignity of the women and their experience in working with the land.[74] (Shiva's role in this transformation would be interesting to trace.) These movements are recovering what Shiva calls "the feminine principle," which preserves and protects *prakriti*—the source of all life.[75]

For Shiva, these women's movements are engaged in preserving biodiversity, both ecologically and culturally. Over two-thirds of the world's natural biodiversity resides in the Third World. Many peasants and tribal peoples depend on that biodiversity for their survival. Moreover, their lifestyles represent a cultural biodiversity that will be lost along with the flora and fauna if the "monoculture" of modern global capitalism is allowed to move unimpeded through these societies. Hence the preservation of biodiversity in both the natural and human worlds becomes of paramount importance for Shiva.[76]

The Role of the Human

Shiva takes her cue for the human role from these women's ecological movements. We too must adopt an attitude toward life that is holistic, noncentralized, participatory rather than dictatorial, and supportive of ecological and cultural diversity. The sustenance of life that these women's movements represent must become the anthem of our culture and an organizing precept of society. Such an attitude will provide an antidote to a patriarchal culture of violence against women and against nature. These women, who are "reclaiming life, its sanctity," in search of liberation, are, for Shiva, lighthouses for society in general. They are struggling to recover a "feminine principle" that will help transform the patriarchal support of "maldevelopment."

What would such a transformation entail? First, growth and productivity would be recast according to the production, rather than the elimination, of life. Second, biodiversity rather than homogeneity, in culture, ecology, and economic models, would become respected and would become a logic of production. This would help ensure pluralism and decentralization. Such an approach would strongly assail the World Trade Organization (WTO) and its precursor, the Global Agreement on Tariffs and Trade (GATT), the World Bank, and the U.S. Trade Act, all of which have acted to legalize the patenting of life-forms, to place a market value on human genetic material, to promote large-scale and ecologically harmful megaprojects, and to represent a "monoculture" financed by First World concerns and enforced by First World capital. As a counter to these forces, Shiva's approach constitutes a shift from what she labels "bio-imperialism to bio-democracy."[77] In short, the human is called to a new quarry—not a human – Earth interaction based on domination, instrumentality, and homogeneity but rather one based on ecology, equity, and diversity.

Contributions and Questions of Ecofeminism

As the above analysis reveals, ecofeminism provides a rich and diverse approach to environmental concerns. As noted at the outset of this chapter, it advocates not a value-neutral approach to environmental and social concerns but an engaged one. In so doing, it turns to the social and natural sciences for an understanding of the interwoven aspects of patriarchy in Western and Third World societies.

Contribution

A Radical Social Ecology

Unlike other approaches to environmental concerns such as deep ecology or the Gaia theory, ecofeminism embraces political economy as well as cultural, religious, and ecological insights. It argues compellingly that only an integration of such categories can lead to a transformed and sustainable future human–Earth relationship. Moreover, because these variables are integrated, ecofeminists are involved in a critique not only of social structures but also of cultural and religious metaphors, images, and social identities. Thus in addition to social analysis, Ruether's critique of ideology proffers the image of "gardener," McFague the metaphor of the "world as God's body," and Shiva the notion of *prakriti*—the source of all life. In this sense ecofeminists helpfully avoid the materialist/idealist split that has derailed much philosophical and sociological discourse.

Consequently, their appeals for change include not only a restructuring of the World Bank, the International Monetary Fund, and domestic environmental policy but also new models of the divine and of human interaction with nature. This points to not only a transformation in our physical and material relationship with nature—that is, how we use and conserve energy, how we treat natural resources, how we produce food, and so on—but also a change in our religious and philosophical consciousness regarding nature.

The broader implications of this integrated agenda are that the rich vein of feminist analysis can no longer be done in isolation from the natural world. Ecofeminists cogently demonstrate that any feminist analysis that does not take into account ecological destruction is both limited and potentially damaging for any socially just and environmentally enhanced future. In short, they show that to be a feminist one has to also be an environmentalist.

The Notion of the Human as Relational

Ecofeminism also offers an important alternative to the atomistic, highly individualistic, and separate self bequeathed to us by modernity. For the ecofeminist, the self is primarily relational: it emerges not as an independent, cloistered self-reliant reality but as an "embedded" reality. This self is not independent of or lord over the natural world but utterly dependent on it and yet capable of defining its own relationship with it. Thus the ecofeminists hold out the notion of mutuality with nature without sacrificing the idea of human responsibility toward nature. Unlike the relationality of deep ecology and the Gaia theory, which makes the human somewhat ancillary and subservient to nature, the ecofeminist notion of relationality develops a distinctive role for the human, one that recognizes the human power to alter and destroy nature. It therefore demands a sense of responsibility, accountability, and self-criticism.

Questions

Is Ecofeminism Gynocentric?

As all ecofeminists agree, patriarchy assigns an essentialism to women as related to nature and therefore inferior to men. Just as nature is to be dominated and controlled by men, so are women. Yet does ecofeminism ascribe to women an essentialism in relation to nature that gives them a superiority? The feminine principle of Shiva as a universal principle to be followed suggests this, as does McFague's maternal God. Do ecofeminists take a hard look at how women's cultures engender and perpetuate patriarchy and how women become agents of ecological destruction? How are women's relationships to nature oppressive and destructive of the Earth? How can ideologies of the feminine contribute to a destruction of nature? More importantly, how are women's forms of power rooted in the domination of nature?

For example, to what extent is women's control of the household—which in Western culture includes the extensive use of toxic cleaning fluids, pesticides, and herbicides—destructive of nature? To what extent has women's consumerism—a partial product of their entry into the workforce and having greater control over the disposal of their income—been harmful of nature? Such questions suggest that ecofeminism would be strengthened if it eschewed essentialist readings of "women" and continued to focus on the complex and myriad relationship of women with the natural world, as indeed Ruether has begun to do.[78] While certainly not opting for the "biology is destiny" argument, I wonder if solidary feminists have adequately dealt with the realities of biology. Certainly, biology is not destiny, but it is reality and has some independence from culturally conditioned patterns.

Does Ecofeminism Romanticize Nature?

In their search for alternative material and philosophical understandings of the human-Earth relationship, ecofeminists, as we have seen, have turned to scientific theories of the natural world. In exploring the Gaia theory, for example, with its emphasis on cooperation rather than competition, Ruether holds up the idea of mutuality as a social goal with a deep connection to natural processes. Shiva proffers the "feminine principle" at work in nature as a paradigm for human interaction with the nonhuman world, and McFague anthropomorphizes nature as the "new poor" in her attempt to incorporate a liberationist theological category. Moreover, both McFague and Ruether view nature as victim; it is "fallen," owing not to any inherent quality of nature but to the rapacious plunder of humanity. Clearly, as the ecofeminists point out, the life-systems of the planet are seriously jeopardized owing to human activity. Yet nature itself is not without its own elements of destruction, loss, and in some cases devastation. Do ecofeminists romanticize the mutuality and harmony of nature while not seriously engaging its violent aspect? While this area is touched on in McFague's work to a certain extent, the question remains: How do we as humans reconcile this notion of nature's violence with this concept of nature's mutuality?

These questions about the role of violence in nature also raise some substantial queries concerning the incorporation of scientific findings in ecofeminist thought. Much of our understanding of the "violence" of nature has been provided by modern scientific observation. From the "big bang," some 13.7 billion years ago, an explosion whose effects we still feel, to the mass slaughter of newly hatched sea tortoises by sea birds as they make their inaugural race to the ocean, nature's violence is systemic and beyond easy ethical categorizations. These observations about the violence of nature indicate that nature is not a neat and tidy affair. While Darwin's interpretation of such activity as "survival of the fittest" contributes to a paradigm of domination, as these authors show, there is nonetheless the residual truth of predator – prey relations that perhaps belies a romanticized understanding of what ecofeminists identify as mutuality and cooperation in nature, which is to be emulated by humans. I think it is helpful to distinguish between thinkers who moved from a socialist feminism into ecology, like Ruether, and those who were primarily concerned with the liberation of women and then moved to the environmental aspect. As is evident, McFague is not engaged in as robust a systematic critique of free-trade capitalism as is Ruether or Shiva.

In fact, it is surprising how little some of these authors, for example, McFague, up till now treat the ponderous impact of industrial capitalism on the environment. Ruether is more sensitive to this point, and Shiva is the only one who addresses it from an agricultural base, showing the sustainability of women's peasant agriculture and the ecological horrors of a free-trade, growth-maximizing, world-capitalist monoculture. This raises the larger question of how seriously these authors take the influence of economic structures on the shaping of human consciousness, which a liberationist perspective takes very seriously.

The Limits of Dualistic Discourse

It appears that the ecofeminist critics are not advocating some sort of monism: they recognize the difference between the two poles in the various dualisms noted above but affirm their interaction and interdependence. The question then arises: Does this exclude altogether a "higher" and "lower" between each pair of poles? Since ecofeminists want "humans" to act responsibly in regard to "nature," they seem to credit humans with the higher faculty of critical intelligence. At the same time, there is no higher and lower when it comes to men and women. In other words, each of these dualisms has its own character: they are not all alike.

It is therefore not helpful to stress only the similarity among the lower poles of these dualisms, by saying for instance that as women are oppressed, so is nature. One must also point to the difference. For humans inevitably consume nature when they eat and drink, while using and "consuming" women is *always* a crime. In other words, while the antidualism discourse has a useful rhetorical function, it also has its limitations. This nuance is seen, for example, in Ruether's notion of the human as gardener, suggesting a managerial "dualism," if you will, between humans and nonhuman nature.

Conclusion

Despite these queries and concerns, ecofeminism remains a vital and engaging theological approach to a political theology of the environment. It embodies a transformative, political dimension informed by liberationist precepts. The equating of the oppression of the poor with the plunder of the Earth reflects the preferential option of the poor that is a defining feature of liberation theology. Moreover, ecofeminism uses the category of solidarity with women in the Third World, as support for the Chipko and Appiko movements shown by Shiva and others illustrates. Here is a concrete commitment to groups struggling to preserve their way of life and their lands. Also, like liberation thought, ecofeminism mines the rich prophetic tradition of the Judeo-Christian heritage (Ruether) and remains self-critical in its approach, using a trial-and-error method and calling for collegiality rather than chauvinism in the theological enterprise. Finally, ecofeminists, like many liberation theologians, see theology as a "second act," the "first act" being solidarity with groups struggling for dignity, freedom from sexism and economic oppression, as well as ecological sustainability.

Of the ecofeminists examined, Vandana Shiva is probably the most sobering and challenging for First World readers. Her critique, coming from the perspective of Third World women and their rejection of a globalizing corporate "monoculture" enforcing a "free-market economy," is a gauntlet cast down for those in the industrialized world.

The Gulf of Mexico Oil Spill: Would the "Precautionary Principle" Have Averted This Disaster?

By Paul Fraumeni

I t's now the largest and most devastating oil spill in U.S. history, even bigger than the infamous Exxon Valdez spill in 1989. The Gulf of Mexico oil spill, caused by an explosion of the Deepwater Horizon oil rig 40 miles south of the Louisiana coastline on April 20, 2010, is coating the waters of the Gulf of Mexico and the marshlands that are home to hundreds of species of birds and marine life.

Professor Stephen Scharper, associate professor of anthropology at the University of Toronto (U of T) Mississauga and at U of T's Centre for Environment, provides perspective on the spill and how it might have been averted.

This is a disaster that is having a double negative impact, isn't it? The fish and wildlife that live in and on the water and wetlands in the Gulf are being devastated and so are the people who make their living in the Gulf of Mexico fishing industry.

I was just reading about "Ring of Fire," a radio program hosted by Robert Kennedy Jr. and Mike Papantonio. They are environmental lawyers who are preparing a class action suit now against BP and they said this is the prime harvesting season in Louisiana—80 percent of fishing happens between now and September. So, with this oil spill, the Louisiana fishing industry is stalled. The fishermen are going out of business. This is a multibillion dollar industry that goes back generations in that region.

In a column you wrote in the Toronto Star *recently, you explored the need for greater adherence to what you call the "precautionary principle" in the case of the Gulf of Mexico oil spill and others like it. What is the "precautionary principle"?*

Precaution is defined as "caution in advance," or "informed prudence," or a term that I used in that article, "preemptive prudence." By using the precautionary principle, you anticipate the harm that may come, based on scientific and other evidence, to the environment and human communities from any kind of activity.

The precautionary principle embodies an expression of the need for decision makers to anticipate harm before it occurs. As I understand it, this notion of precaution was first introduced in environmental activity in Germany in the 1970s. What it says is you don't need absolute scientific evidence that an activity is going to bring harm; you can have suggestive scientific evidence. Therefore, you enact mitigation prevention and put in safeguards to deal with any possible effects that could occur.

For example, we use the precautionary principle with automobiles. We know that driving a car or truck can be dangerous, so we mitigate through safety features such as seatbelts and airbags.

Finally, the precautionary principle builds a fundamentally different notion of nature and the place of the human in it. The principle realizes that the human, first of all, is not lord and master over nature, that we can't technologically fix all of our messes, that all the king's horses and all the king's men can't put the Gulf of Mexico back together again, and that we can actually destroy ecosystems and our technology can't bring them back. So this precautionary principle is building on the dependency the human has on nature, rather than the mastery the human thinks it has over nature.

Can you provide an example of how not using the precautionary principle has resulted in environmental damage?

There was the case of rivers that were flooded by Hydro Quebec in the 1970s when dams were being constructed near James Bay.

Hydro Quebec didn't anticipate that when they flooded that much area and had that much organic material decomposing, in the process the microorganisms that decompose the organic matter would produce mercury as waste matter. This led to incredible rates of mercury poisoning among the Cree people who were eating the fish from these rivers. This had not been foreseen when Hydro Quebec undertook the project.

If Hydro Quebec had invoked the precautionary principle, various experts could have predicted that something like this might happen and, thus, precautionary measures would have been taken.

Actually, this principle has been in place in international declarations, including the Earth Summit in Rio de Janeiro in 1992. Principal 15 of the Rio Declaration states,

> In order to protect the environment, the precautionary approach shall be widely applied by states according to their capabilities. Where there are threats of serious or irreversible damage, lack of full scientific certainty shall not be used as a reason for postponing cost effective measures to prevent environmental degradation.

It also was adopted by the European Union and in the UN Charter for Nature. Parks Canada has also included the precautionary principle in some of its planning. So it's becoming more codified in environmental policy making and decision makers at all levels of government are using it increasingly.

And what's interesting is that it does not demand conclusive scientific evidence. The precaution can be suggestive and not conclusive. In a sense, this reverses a way of thinking that is popular in North America, particularly the United States, where we say, "If it can be done, it should be done. If we can do it technologically, let's go for it."

By using the precautionary principle, you are putting the brakes on that kind of thinking.

How does this precautionary principle relate specifically to the Gulf of Mexico oil spill?

There is a lot about this oil spill that is disturbing.

It has been revealed that the Mineral Management Service, the group responsible for oversight of drilling in the United States, is also the group responsible for encouraging offshore oil drilling and, indeed, getting the royalties from it. So this group has a conflicting purpose. Thankfully, the Obama administration has just moved that these powers be separated. And the MMS director just resigned.

The *New York Times* and other news organizations have written that this group has been compromised. Members of the group who were supposed to do inspections have received various gifts from the oil companies. In some cases, according to the *Sacramento Bee*, the companies were allowed to write their own inspection certificates and reports.

As for the precautionary principle, it's becoming clear in this case that the precautionary principle was not part of the negotiations and this emerged even before the Obama administration, particularly with former Vice President Dick Cheney's role in the Bush administration. The three groups involved in the Deepwater Horizon oil rig are BP, Trans Ocean, which did the construction, and Halliburton, and, of course, Cheney was a major player in Halliburton in the 1990s.

According to Mike Papantonio and Ed Schultz of MSNBC, permits were not even required in building and installing this oil rig, and the government oversight was removed. According to Papantonio and Schultz, this kind of rig could not have been built off of European waters because there they require this blowout device to be regulated. Europe also requires an emergency failsafe capping system where, if anything goes wrong at the deep level, the oil well is shut down. It's required in Europe but was waived in the United States. So government regulation and the precautionary principle were both steamrolled in this case.

The second thing here is the chemical being used to disperse the oil, Corexit, that is now deep in the water and which has moved into the wetlands of Louisiana. The Environmental Protection Agency has finally intervened and said this is a harmful chemical, it's never been used at that deep water level, it's not known what the effects are, so stop using it. I read in the *New York Times* that BP has said no, they still want to use it. So now they're in a negotiation.

So who has the right to protect the common good? This is a question that this particular spill is raising.

The outrage from the public and the media attention over this spill both seem to be greater than I remember with the Exxon Valdez disaster off the coast of Alaska in 1989. What do you think?

Part of the reaction is that this spill is affecting a huge swath of the American population and potentially other countries, such as Cuba and other countries in the Caribbean and it could go up the U.S. east coast. The Exxon Valdez was a huge spill that caused massive damage to the ecology and environment, but it was spilling onto an area that was largely not inhabited by people.

But the Gulf spill is hitting a traditional mainland area that affects millions of people and billions of dollars worth of business in the fishing industry and in related industries, such as tourism. So it brings into the mix what we call "social ecology." "Deep ecology" celebrates wilderness and the intrinsic value of nature. "Social ecology," on the other hand, looks at how environmental accidents affect people and social communities. What's interesting with this spill is that it blends concerns from social ecology with deep ecology. And that's probably another reason that it is getting so much media attention.

There are about 3,000 oil rigs in the Gulf right now. You have oil rigs in Europe with more restrictions than in the U.S. But they are still making money. I've read that BP made $4 billion last year. So they're not hurting. But what this says is just as we need a permit to change our driveways, oil companies need to go through a more stringent permit process to punch a hole in the bottom of the Gulf of Mexico.

Actually, Shell called for a universal standard that all companies have to adhere to a few years ago. And that's what we need. You make it a universal regulation that all have to have this blowout device, all have to have the failsafe choke mechanism, as certain parts of Europe require. According to Mike Papantonio, this blowout device costs only $500,000. Not a big expense for BP and not a big expense when you think of the billions of dollars of damage that is being done.

Will this be a watershed? Will this disaster actually, in time, change things for the better?

It's too early to tell. Some people will continue to see these spills as necessary evils in the quest to not have to depend on foreign oil in North America. It's going to be a big power play that way and the media will play an important role on both sides.

What might turn people around, however, is the fragility of the Gulf of Mexico ecosystem.

The *Globe and Mail*'s Alanna Mitchell has written that through the increased carbon we create, the oceans are becoming acidic and making it more difficult for coral reefs and major micro-organisms and plankton to breed.

She says that in the Gulf, there is a huge dead zone caused by the fertilizer run-off that comes through the Mississippi Delta. It's gargantuan and the fish have been avoiding it. With this oil spill, she says, the fish are trapped between a fertilizer cesspool and a murky oil deathbed. So the fish are trying to navigate between these two colossal deathtraps.

This kind of data and realization might result in a watershed moment where people realize that these are compromised oceans already. Still, Obama has authorized it all the way up the coast to Delaware and off the Alaskan shore. Even after the Gulf spill the government has granted permits to drillers. That is wrong. It's ludicrous. I am heartened to hear that President Obama has admitted his error in part and has now called for a six-month moratorium on coastal drilling.

This is where we have to put pressure on decision makers. In Canada, it's potentially the same situation with the offshore oil rigs near Newfoundland and proposals for drilling in the Beaufort Sea. This could happen here very easily if we do not demand stringent precautionary measures.

Questions to Ponder
and Exercises to Consider

1. Scharper asks the question "What on Earth Are We Doing?" to underline the social-global dimensions to the Anthropocene, such as rapid urbanization, widespread pollution, skyrocketing population, rapacious mining, and the excessive combustion of fossil fuels. In fact, the point is not to change the world singlehandedly, but to engage in a communal vision and action that fosters peace and harmony with the entire planet. Nevertheless, as individuals we are not exempt from taking stock of our own relationship with the planet and asking, "What on Earth am *I* doing?"

   For example, in "Born Again: Liberation Theology," Scharper quotes Ivan Petrella, who notes, "it would take an additional yearly investment of $6 billion to assure basic education for everyone, while $8 billion is spent annually on cosmetics in the U.S." and "$9 billion of investment would take care of clean water, while $11 billion a year is spent on ice cream in Europe."

   In "The Gulf of Mexico Oil Spill," Scharper points out that "through the increased carbon we create, the oceans are becoming acidic and making it more difficult for coral reefs and major microorganisms and plankton to breed." Scharper also notes that in the Gulf of Mexico there is a huge dead zone caused by the fertilizer run-off from farms that comes through the Mississippi Delta, creating a "fertilizer cesspool." Dead zones can be found not only across the United States, but in Canada and, indeed, the world.

Take a moment to reflect on your own human–human and human–non-human relationship or, simply, your lifestyle—how you eat, pray, learn, vote, communicate, play, travel, shop, consume, and so on. How might these actions be impacting on local ecosystems, natural animal habitats, rising sea levels, and the pollution of water, air, and land? To what extent is your lifestyle a reflection of the larger habits of your community? Your nation? Western culture? What are five lifestyle changes you personally would find difficult to change? What are five lifestyle changes you think our greater society would find difficult to change?

2. Ecofeminists find that the logic used to justify the domination of humans by gender, ethnic or class status is the same logic used to justify the domination over nature. This exercise is designed to examine this theory, using the chart below. Based on the readings, choose an issue for each of the categories found in the left column in the grid chart. It can be any issue, really. For example, a gender issue could be access to education for females, equity pay, roles at home or work, or specific issues such as female genital mutilation. For ethnic and class, it could be similar issues: access to education, equity pay, roles at home or work, or specific issues such as requirements to immigrate to your country. For environment, it could be any number of things, from pollution issues, public transit issues, or climate change to carbon tax or cap-and-trade issues. Whatever issues you choose, answer the corresponding questions along the top column. (You can do this exercise alone or within a small group.)

When you have completed the chart, reflect on any patterns you might see. In what way might politics, values, and control of decision making be linked? Do any of the interlocking dualisms that ecofeminists speak about reveal themselves in this grid?

	Who controls the decision making on the issue?	What are the values and beliefs held about this issue?	What, if any, are the economic issues?	What are the present local, regional, and national policies on the issues?
A gender issue:				
An ethnic issue:				
A class status issue:				
An environment issue:				

3. In "O Ye of Little Eco-faith," Scharper speaks of the rise of "the profound rereading of our life and culture spawned by our ecological profligacy." Back in Section I, in "Truth, Lies, and Broadcasting in Canada," Scharper also speaks about the watering down of truth telling that is increasingly apparent in the media.

   This raises questions on where we go for information in "rereading life and culture." What are your sources of information on issues on the environmental crisis and deepening global poverty? What videos, documentaries, books, or articles (news, magazine, or journal) dealing with these issues have informed you? Who edits the news content of those sources? Do you engage in any communal discussions on the matter? What methods do you use to ensure that you remain as well-informed as you can be on these subjects?

SECTION III

Redeeming—A Creative Space
for New Life-giving Relationships

Introduction

If, as Andre Gunder Frank maintains,
one does not have development without underdevelopment,
then arguably one does not have sustainable development
without "unsustainable underdevelopment."

Stephen Bede Scharper

It's not just about sacrifice, but about making a space
for a novel and possibly enhanced way of life.
It may also hold hidden harvests for the spiritual and material
well-being, not only of our families and nation,
but of our larger household, the Earth.

Stephen Bede Scharper

To create a world of life-giving relationships will require nurturing an imaginative, creative space where we can begin to address the very difficult ethical questions we have encountered in the previous sections. Our aim is no less than the realization of a renewed, transformed *ontology*, a philosophical term Scharper employs to denote a "new way of being human." It is also within this creative space that we can conceive the co-penetration of the human and non-human world, which means we can no longer discuss environmental issues without also examining the economic, social, and political dimensions of ecology in their present and historical contexts.

While this might sound like a near-impossible task, it's hardly a task we can avoid, as Scharper suggests. We will need to liberate ourselves in a concrete manner from our present destructive ways of being if we wish to nurture a new life-giving relationship with the world. We cannot do this, however, without first learning to set limits, make sacrifices, and apply restrictions to ourselves, thereby redeeming ourselves and facilitating our falling in love with the Earth.

Scharper suggests that we can begin this journey of transformation by learning "to think like a mountain." He is taking his cue here from Aldo Leopold, whose thinking plays an important role in Scharper's ethic. Writing in the mid-20th century, Leopold instigates what he considers to be a logical step in the evolution of ethics when he suggests that we learn to think and see things from the point of view of the biotic community.

When you think of it, what Leopold is suggesting is profound: he posits that human ethics should embrace the "integrity, stability, and beauty of the biotic community." To get to that point, however, he suggests we begin by thinking like a mountain, as well as a wolf, a stream and a tree.

How, you might ask, is it possible to think like a mountain?

This is a good question, as it's seldom clear what specifically constitutes the integrity, stability, and beauty of the biotic community, let alone a mountain. Scharper contends that it requires analogous thinking, which is an idea he gets from Thomas Berry, another person whose writings play an important role in Scharper's thought. Normally, when we speak of the "rights" of a human and the rights of the other-than-human, we have trouble assessing the two because of their apparent differences, and too often end with human rights trumping the rights of the non-human. However, if we employ "rights" as an analogous term, we see similarities and differences. In this way, we can say that a mountain has rights. The mountain, however, does not have human rights, because human rights would be no good for a mountain. A mountain needs mountain rights. Similarly, plants need plant rights, birds need bird rights, rivers need river rights, and so on.

If we are indeed a "communion of subjects" rather than a "collection of objects" to be bought, sold, used and discarded, as Berry contends, and "just plain citizens" of the larger natural community, as Leopold argues, it is incumbent upon us to consult the mountain and wolf before deciding upon our own actions. However, within this communal discussion with the natural world, Scharper includes the insights from liberation theology. The Union Carbide disaster that Scharper discusses in "Option for the Poor and Option for the Earth: Toward a Sustainable Solidarity" is a vivid example of why this approach is crucial. It reminds us that a majority of human beings are not even granted the status of citizen, let alone "plain citizen." We see, then, how the rejection of the status of "citizenship" to humans and the natural world are interrelated.

Conversely, if we were to look at the world through the "prisms of the poor," while simultaneously thinking like a mountain, we learn to locate the entire world human population squarely in the centre of deliberations on environmental issues. Suddenly, as we first discussed in the introduction to this book, there is no environment "out there," apart from the human. We *are part of* the environment.

In fostering a creative space in our minds and hearts, Scharper believes, we become better situated to take on the pressing and difficult ethical questions: can we talk about sustainable development of peoples in the global South while continuing our unsustainable development of relatively few peoples in the global North? How can we change our lifestyles so that we are no longer in the driver's seat of the destruction of Earth? Need we be so afraid of change? Of sacrifice? Can we ignore the fact that too often, even our environmental projects as well as our social and economic development projects deflect the resultant burdens onto already marginalized populations?

The writings in this section address these questions in concrete ways. The shorter articles touch upon those parts of our lives that are—to many of us and, in some cases, to all of us—inescapable: marriage, death, eating, driving, and celebrating. However, as in the case of "On Sacrifice, Spirituality, and Silver Linings," redeeming ourselves need not be viewed as a dark journey that is bereft of joy; there can be "unforeseen benefits, silver linings" that enter our lives. Scharper believes the resulting relationships we will foster by being in communion with all of creation, and the love we will nurture with the Earth, will outweigh any supposed disadvantages.

In this light, it is fitting that this section features "From Community to Communion," Scharper's chapter on the "natural city." Today, more people live in urban than in rural areas. For the entire history of the human race, until recently, the opposite was true: most humans lived in rural settings. Given that in the coming decades, all of the world's population growth is expected to take place in urban areas, and given that the benefits of urbanization are often not equally enjoyed by all segments of the population, the city could represent the most vital creative space for defining our vocation as a species in the decades to come.

From Corpse to Compost

So, you have spent your whole life trying to decrease your ecological footprint, recycling cans and bottles, avoiding pesticides in your garden, biking and using public transit as much as possible, and helping others value nature.

Now, as you reach the sunset of life, the thought of filling yourself with toxic embalming fluid before going into an expensive, hardwood casket, or contributing to greenhouse gases through cremation, doesn't quite sit right. Is there a "green" burial alternative, you wonder?

If Janet McCausland has her way, the answer here in Canada will soon be, "You bet!"

McCausland is the executive director of the Toronto-based Natural Burial Association, and her mission is to provide an environmentally friendly alternative to conventional burials in Canada. She espouses "low-impact burials," those that, according to the association brochure, "reduce energy and resource consumption, are less toxic, conserve water, and include materials which are locally produced in a sustainable manner."

While they are just beginning in Canada, McCausland says green burials are increasingly popular in the United Kingdom, which has more than 200 natural burial grounds, as well as New Zealand and the U.S., which has seen natural burial sites sprout up in California, New

York, Florida, and South Carolina. She is working to ensure that such burials will be available here in Canada in the near future.

For Mary Woodsen, president of Green Springs Natural Cemetery Association ("Save a forest. Plant yourself.") in upstate New York, the ecological cost of contemporary, conventional burials is steep, forming a part of the ecological crisis few ever consider.

"On average," she says, "a U.S. cemetery buries 1,000 gallons of embalming fluid, 97.5 tons of steel, 2,028 tons of concrete, and 56,250 board feet of high quality tropical hardwood in just one acre of green. And then there's the tons of fertilizers, pesticides, and water not to mention emissions like CO2 nitrates, ozone, soot, and more that it takes to keep cemeteries looking well-manicured."

And if you think cremation is more environmentally benign, Woodsen says, think again.

"Each cremation," Woodsen claims, "releases between .8 and 5.9 grams of mercury as bodies are burned. This amounts to between 1,000 and 7,800 pounds of mercury released each year in the U.S."

The alternative, "natural burial," Woodsen describes as "letting nature take its course: no embalming fluid, simple biodegradable caskets, environmentally responsible care of the land, low-density burials, a natural return to the earth, natural stone markers, flush with the earth, or commemorative plantings of native trees and shrubs."

According to the Natural Burial Association, which works co-operatively with the Green Burial Council in the U.S. and the Natural Death Centre in the U.K., natural burial grounds are "green spaces of beauty and ecological renewal." They utilize native species to provide refuge to birds and butterflies, "and groves and wild meadows" to provide solace for the bereaved.

For McCausland, natural burial grounds are also an original way of creating and preserving green spaces, often near urban cores. "One of our dreams," she says, "is to develop brownfields (abandoned industrial and commercial sites) into natural burial grounds."

Natural interment may indeed be an increasingly preferred spiritual alternative as more religious groups engage in ecological reflection and renewal. The Canadian Forum on Religion and Ecology and the Faith and the Common Good Project in Canada are but two examples of hundreds of religious environmental initiatives worldwide, and as their members are involved in the religious rituals surrounding burials, the green alternative may increase along with their ecological awareness. For McCausland, a Unitarian, the environment has long been a part of her spirituality.

A vegetarian, McCausland sees a direct connection between her advocacy for natural burials and the Seventh Principle of the Unitarian Universalists, which posits "respect for the interdependent web of all existence of which we are a part."

The natural death movement also invokes the spiritual qualities of humility and charity. Millions of Christians have heard the humbling reminder on Ash Wednesday that they are "dust" and "unto dust" they shall return, and the idea of a simple, non-polluting, non-ostentatious burial invokes the notion that we, as humans, are "just plain citizens" of the land, rather than its reigning lords and masters.

Such a burial also suggests that in dying we also have a last chance at giving, not only through organ donation, but also through the return to the soil of our very bodies, which in death, through non-toxic decomposition, can help engender new life.

A redemptive thought to carry to the grave.

The Bride Wore ... Green

As Spring sprouts around us, thoughts turn to gardens, flowers, birdsong ... and weddings.

Weddings are grand occasions—and getting grander. Each year, according to *Wedding Bells* magazine, Canadian couples plan to spend about $17,300 on their big day, but eventually fork out, on average, $23,000. That's a lot of nuptials.

Let's face it. Weddings have become consumerist celebrations, with hefty ecological footfalls. And unfettered consumerism is a major roadblock to an eco-friendly lifestyle. So, if you and your betrothed are an environmentally concerned couple, what to do?

Can you have a big bash without making a big gash in the planet?

People are waking up to the so-called eco-crisis and, as a result, are trying to read the major moments of their lives through a green lens.

Funerals, for example, are now being greened through the eco-burial movement, which sheds tropical hardwood caskets and polluting embalming and cremation processes for simple, unadorned "plantings" of our bodies.

So it is with weddings. Many who seek eco-friendly matrimony are now aided by writers such as Emily Elizabeth Anderson, author of *Eco-Chic Weddings*.

Marrying the 3 Rs—Reduce, Reuse, Recycle—with a quest for fair trade, non-sweatshop bridal attire, Anderson argues that much of the greening of matrimony can be quite simple. Using in-season flowers, for example, is cheaper and reduces the environmental cost of shipping in non-local blooms. Avoiding the "save-the date" cards saves some trees, and steering clear of "one-time use" dresses, shoes, and glassware is also gentler on the Earth. Those who see their union as a sacred event are incorporating nature into their services. At one recent wedding, the couple chose to hold their ceremony outdoors, read Scripture that accented creation, and substituted birdseed for rice for their post-ceremony shower.

In a sense, for those with spiritual sensibility, eco-weddings are an invitation to include additional 3 Rs. The first R is "Reciprocate." In a marriage, partners are called on to "give back," especially in hard times, as the human family is called in environmental contexts to give back to and not just take from creation.

The second R is "Rejoice." Creation, like wedding revellers, also goes "gaga," from the brilliant formation of stars to a sea of alpine wildflowers in bloom. An eco-marriage asks how to connect with the creative rejoicing of nature in a mutually life-giving way.

Finally, there's "Respect," the bedrock of a sound marriage, even during fractious times. An eco-marriage unites this mutual respect to respect for creation itself, and vows to never abuse the natural world.

Greening your wedding, then, can be an occasion to consume less, and be consumed more, by the creativity and celebrative joy of the natural world.

From Community to Communion:
The Natural City in Biotic and
Cosmological Perspective

A thing is right when it tends to preserve the integrity,
stability and beauty of the biotic community.

Aldo Leopold

The universe is a communion of subjects,
not a collection of objects.

Thomas Berry

The above epigraphs might appear incongruous for a reflection on urban environmentalism. After all, Aldo Leopold (1887–1948), who provided the foundation for wildlife ecology and intellectual grist for deep ecology, is not known for his writings on the urban condition. And Thomas Berry (1914–2009), cultural historian and "geologian," has focused on the "new cosmology" and the awesome wonder of the expanding universe more than on the ecology of cities. Yet both of these environmental pathfinders, with their profound insights into the intricately integrated community of life, proffer insights at once incisive and challenging for those seeking environmental integrity within an urban context.

In this chapter, I wish to reflect upon the implications of Leopold's "land ethic" as well as Thomas Berry's idea of a universal "communion of subjects" for the notion of ecological integrity within cities. As the ecological consequences of sprawling and increasingly poverty-stricken urban spaces are addressed with more frequency in literature on "sustainability," there are signs that a significant ethical transformation concerning human relationships with the natural world is emerging in the process. The natural city concept is, in a sense, part of this "evolution of ethics," to borrow Aldo Leopold's term, and holds the potential of bringing together pragmatic, ontological, and cosmological issues in cogent ways as it attempts to imagine a new way of being urban in the world.

Town and Country

The town and country, urban–rural divide is arguably the most nettlesome Gordian knot in urban environmental thinking, and may be as old as the first human settlements. This diremption is perhaps as dust-strewn as the ancient remains of Athens, when persons began to build and inhabit the polis and distinguish themselves from the cosmos. As theorist Raymond Williams has shown in his rich literary account of this nature–city divide, from the pastoral vistas of Virgil's *Eclogues* (37 BCE) through D. H. Lawrence's dichotomy of mine and farm in *Sons and Lovers* (1913), this separation has been solidified not only in the literary imagination, but in the economic, cultural, and political practice of the West in both uplifting and oppressive ways.[1] In probing this literature through a lens profoundly critical of industrial capitalism, yet with a deep-seated, almost visceral appreciation of its urban achievements, Williams unearths the social background to many of our assumed nostrums concerning the separation of not only town and country, but also many other concomitant dualisms, such as city dweller and peasant, metropole and backwater, enlightened and benighted. He writes:

> On the country has gathered the idea of a natural way of life: of peace, innocence, and simple virtue. On the city has gathered the idea of an achieved centre: of learning, communication,

light. Powerful hostile associations have also developed: on the city as a place of noise, worldliness, and ambition; on the country as a place of backwardness, ignorance, limitation. A contrast between country and city, as fundamental ways of life, reaches back into classical times.[2]

Williams highlights the varied complexities behind such assumed dichotomies, and explores how the nature of both city and country was profoundly altered by industrialization, a transformation portrayed in novels such as Richard Llewellyn's 1939 work, *How Green Was My Valley*, a poignant story of ecological and family disintegration in an industrial mining village in Wales.

It was just such a gulf between town and country as it emerged through the advent of industrialization that early visionaries of urban planning, such as Ebenezer Howard, strove to bridge in their early city schemas. In his 1898 classic, *Garden Cities of Tomorrow*, Howard attempted to fuse town and country into a unique amalgam, using the metaphor of the "three magnets": town, country, and town–country. The latter, he averred, blended the best of both realities. In Howard's gaze, this urban vision was nuptial in nature: "Town and country *must be married* and out of this joyous union will spring a new hope, a new life, a new civilization."[3]

For Howard, marital bliss became the utopian template of sustainability; he hoped to create a "garden city" that consummated such a union of rural and urban life. His efforts met with some pragmatic success, leading to the creation of the Garden Cities Association and his own involvement in the development of the towns of Letchworth (1911) and Welwyn (1928) outside of London, based on his precepts.[4]

Building on Howard's hoped-for town–country marriage in the wake of the rapid industrialization of urban areas, the dynamic social critic and urban theorist Lewis Mumford also sought a deeper interconnection between urban and rural life. In *The Culture of Cities*, he states, "City is a fact in nature, like a cave, a run of mackerel, or an ant heap. But it is also a conscious work of art."[5] Like Scottish urban critic Patrick Geddes, Mumford was interested in furthering Howard's notion of the "garden city" as a response to the underside of industrialized urban living: overcrowding, poor sanitation, pollution, and accompanying public health concerns.[6] For Mumford, cities, as both organic realities and sites of human artistic expression, were a type of societal artistry, and had to move beyond both the "will to power" and the "will to profit." Such proclivities, in his estimation, led to wide social and economic imbalances, and yielded fulsome slums and ghettos, which he describes as "crystallization of chaos" and forms of "social derangement." Mumford's comments on the newly industrial urban landscape reveal an almost plaintive, nostalgic tone:

> The new cities grew up without the benefit of coherent social knowledge or orderly social effort; they lacked the useful urban folkways of the middle ages or the confident esthetic command of the Baroque period: indeed, a seventeenth-century Dutch peasant, in his little village, knew more about the art of living in communities than a nineteenth-century municipal councilor in London or Berlin.[7]

The task of the urban planner and indeed all "artists" of the urban canvas, Mumford claimed, must be to reject a "stale cult of death," such as the architects of both German and Italian fascism had produced, and erect instead a "cult of life." (Here, interestingly, Mumford echoes the ancient Hebrew exhortation: "Let the heavens and the earth listen, that they may be witnesses against you. I have placed before you life and death, blessing and curse, therefore choose life, so that you and your descendants may live" [Deuteronomy 30:19–20].)

Deeper in the 20th century, Scottish-born urban theorist Ian L. McHarg also attempted to reconstitute the city within nature. His influential work, *Design with Nature* (1969), sold a quarter of a million copies and has been credited, along with Rachel Carson's *Silent Spring* (1962), with helping to foster the modern environmental movement.[8] By encouraging architects, urban planners, and municipal policy makers to integrate the natural world more systematically within their planning, McHarg sounded a tocsin over the emerging urban sprawl and its odious social and ecological consequences.[9]

Noting the disturbing shift from cities to metropolitan areas in North America, McHarg chastised suburban planners for failing to see that "a subdivision is not a community," nudging them to take detailed ecological inventories involving floodplains, marshes, aquifers, and woodlands before breaking ground for new development.

In anticipation of what would become standardized environmental assessments and impact statements, he exhorts:

> Let us ask the land where are the best sites ... in the quest for survival, success and fulfillment, the ecological view offers an invaluable insight. It shows the way for the man who would be the enzyme of the biosphere—its steward, enhancing the creative fit of man-environment, realizing man's design of nature.[10]

The Environmental Movement Meets the City

As the tide of environmental concern began to rise during the 1960s and early 1970s, it began to spill over into North American governmental legislation, urban planning, and social policy, leading to new environmental approaches in a wide array of areas, including architecture, energy, housing, social equity, land restoration, economic development, transportation, policy formation, governance, and myriad others.

Such developments highlighted the dearth of serious environmental consideration that had marked the erection of modern cities. Stephen M. Wheeler and Timothy Beatley succinctly survey this "denatured" legacy:

> Although landscape architects and park designers have long sought to bring nature into cities, this need was often ignored by developers and the nascent city planning profession in the nineteenth and twentieth centuries. Engineers and developers filled in or paved over streams, wetlands, and shorelines to make way for urban expansion. Highways or railroad lines cut many cities off from their waterfronts. Hills were leveled and native vegetation removed. Landowners plotted lots and built roads without considering the implications for wildlife, native

plant species, or human recreation. With the advent of central heating, electric lighting, air conditioning, long-distance food transport, or huge dams and pipelines bringing water from hundreds of miles away, urban residents became well insulated from nature in all its forms, and even from the limitations of climate and local geography.[11]

Cities had become *de facto* monuments to modern humanity's self-understanding as "master" and "conqueror" of nature, a stance that envisioned nature as separate from the human, serving the human project as both booty to be exploited and backdrop to be decorated with human desires.

Among those championing a deeper understanding of the foundational relationships between cities and nature emerging out of the environmental movement was Anne Whiston Spirn, professor of architecture at the University of Pennsylvania. Her 1984 book, *The Granite Garden*, argued that cities should be viewed as something wholly within, rather than beyond or above, the natural world. Building on the insights of both Mumford and McHarg, Spirn began to view the omnipresence of nature within city limits:

> Nature pervades the city, forging bonds between the city and the air, earth, water, and living organisms within and around it … The city must be recognized as part of nature and designed accordingly. The city, the suburbs, and the countryside must be viewed as a single, evolving system within nature, as must every individual park and building within that larger whole.[12]

Spirn's innovative work on community, albeit a managed one, was continued in the work of Peter Calthorpe, Andres Duany, Elizabeth Plater-Zyberk, and other founders of "new urbanism," which can be viewed as fostering sustainable living by creating smaller, pedestrian-friendly, and resource-efficient living spaces.[13] For example, reflecting the utopian aspirations of Mumford and McHarg, urban designer Peter Calthorpe wrote about the new urbanist vision in his 1993 book, *The Next American Metropolis: Ecology, Community, and the American Dream*, which he describes as "a search for a paradigm that combines the utopian ideal of an integrated and heterogeneous community with the realities of our time—the imperatives of ecology, equity, technology, and the relentless force of inertia ... Quite simply, we need towns rather than sprawl."[14]

Ecological integration, in short, has become a *sine qua non* of theoretical reflections on how ideal cities should be both envisioned and organized. Yet, the nature of that integration, its underlying understanding of the place of the human within not only the biotic community but also the unfolding cosmos, remains at times unexplored in such urban projections and planning. Although McHarg, Mumford, Spirn, and the new urbanists were constructively and creatively moving away from the nature–urban divide, their work remained problematic in its depiction of the human. While seeking to more deeply commingle the human and the natural in their cityscapes, and eschew the noxious elements of sprawl and suburbanization, these theorists still depicted the human as "gardener," "steward," manager, or town builder.

While these metaphors are assuredly welcome advances over notions of the human as conqueror, overlord, and domineering master, they nonetheless imply a controlling, supervisory, and, by extension, superior vantage point for the human in relation to the overall ecosystem of urban areas. At a philosophical level, they also appear to embrace the modern or Enlightenment anthropocentric subject at the centre of reality. Consequently, they appear able to relate to the natural world only as something other than, or less than, human. This modern subject remains circumscribed in terms of its ethical relationships with the natural world. It stands largely as an independent, rather than as a wholly contingent, self, and does not acknowledge the fact that a mountain, watershed, or wolf may not approve of its actions. While this paradigm can assist the human in becoming a better manager, a more benevolent steward, or a more sensitive gardener, and can facilitate a critical perspective on its own epistemological lineage, it ultimately cannot incorporate or acknowledge, in either ecological or ethical terms, its integral relationship with non-human nature.

It is here that the thought of environmental theorist Aldo Leopold marks both an ontological and an epistemological watershed. Leopold's "land ethic"—briefly defined, as indicated by the chapter's epigraph, as the maintenance of "the integrity, stability, and beauty of the biotic community"—challenges not simply the town and country divide, but the modern split between human and non-human nature. This ethic questions not only the cultural and historical dimensions of this divide but also its ethical premises by positing the existence of a deep inter-relationship between humans and non-humans through the concept of the biotic community. Ecology and ethics walk hand in hand, as it were, throughout Leopold's philosophical writings, which intimate that there is not only an ecological but also an ethical web of life. Such a radical co-penetration of the human and non-human is what in part renders his work so groundbreaking (or, more aptly, given his accent on the energy circuit of dirt, soil revealing).

Aldo Leopold: "Thinking Like a Mountain" in the Concrete Jungle

After three decades of working assiduously in the area of game management and wildlife ecology with various U.S. governmental agencies, including vigorous leadership in state-sponsored wolf eradi-cation programs, Aldo Leopold came to a sobering conclusion. Upon seeing, year after year, wolfless lands spawn burgeoning deer herds that first denuded wildlands and subsequently succumbed to starvation, Leopold had a type of metanoia. He began to discern that the purpose of conservation lay not in protecting or promoting individual animals, such as deer, by eliminating predators and thus producing a "shootable surplus." Rather, taking an ecosystem approach, he viewed conserva-tion more as a labour of "preserving health" rather than "managing game," recognizing the inherent value and vitality of ecosystems and thus attempting to support "the widest possible realm in which natural processes might seek their own equilibrium."[15]

Sitting down to pen his essay "Thinking like a Mountain" in April 1944, Leopold recounts a key experience that served as a catalyst for his altered conservation approach. Recalling his experience as a government slayer of wolves, which he at one time referred to as "varmints," Leopold speaks of another reality that might not deem such killing an optimal idea:

> In those days we had never heard of passing up a chance to kill a wolf. In a second we were pumping lead into the pack, but with more excitement than accuracy; how to aim a steep downhill shot is always confusing. When our rifles were empty, the old wolf was down, and a pup was dragging a leg into impassable side-rocks. We reached the old wolf in time to watch a fierce green fire dying in her eyes. I realized then, and have known ever since, that there was something new to me in those eyes—something known only to her and to the mountain. I was young then, and full of trigger-itch; I thought that because fewer wolves meant more deer, that no wolves would mean hunters' paradise. But after seeing the green fire die, I sensed that neither the wolf nor the mountain agreed with such a view.[16]

The "green fire" of the fading wolf helped give rise to the intimation that both wolf and mountain had notions about wildlife management that didn't involve brutal eradication of species. "Green fire" and "thinking like a mountain" thus became cogent metaphors for Leopold's emerging ecological ethic and his speculations concerning a potential agency, an alternative wisdom tradition, as it were, existing within non-human nature. The cozy thinking of a commodity-based, comfort zone economy, which perceives the natural world as merely an instrument to human ease, is questioned, for Leopold, by the wolf's howl, heard by the mountain but rarely by humans:

> We all strive for safety, prosperity, comfort, long life, and dullness. The deer strives with his supple legs, the cowman with trap and poison, the statesman with pen, the most of us with machines, votes, and dollars, but it all comes to the same thing: peace in our time. A measure of success in this is all well enough, and perhaps is a requisite to objective thinking, but too much safety seems to yield only danger in the long run. Perhaps this is behind Thoreau's dictum: "In wildness is the

salvation of the world." Perhaps this is the hidden meaning in the howl of the wolf, long known among mountains, but seldom perceived among men.[17]

Leopold, who had at one time embodied all the traits of the master, professional nature manager, now saw his role, and indeed that of the human species as a whole, not as conqueror and director, but as just "plain member and citizen" of the biotic community. This became, for him, the basis of a "land ethic" and changed the role of *Homo sapiens* from conqueror of the land-community to plain member and citizen of it. Leopold continues:

> It implies respect for his fellow-members, and also respect for the community as such. In human history, we have learned (I hope) that the conqueror role is eventually self-defeating. Why? Because it is implicit in such a role that the conqueror knows, *ex cathedra*, just what makes the community clock tick, and just what and who is valuable, and what and who is worthless, in community life. It always turns out that he knows neither, and this is why his conquests eventually defeat themselves.[18]

At the heart of Leopold's biotic approach is the recognition that in conquest there is always eventual defeat—thus, the human, as plain citizen, seeks not to master the natural world, but to inhabit it as a responsible, participatory member. The human, like any citizen in a democracy, might assume a special leadership role for a time within the biotic community, yet such a temporal service role would ultimately be for the benefit of the larger community and the common good, not for personal gain.

For Leopold, the extension of human ethics to embrace the "integrity, stability, and beauty of the biotic community" is a logical step in the evolution of ethics. Part of this evolution includes the incorporation of an affective dimension to environmental ethical discourse, encouraging the development of an "ecological conscience" that engenders "love, respect, and admiration for the land."[19] In other words, Leopold is proposing much more than rational best practices when it comes to land use. He is, in fact, claiming an ethics of the heart, one rooted in love as much as reason and incorporating awe-filled admiration as much as rational argumentation. This sense of beauty in nature, and deep admiration for its mysteries, is not ancillary but constitutive of Leopold's land ethic.

Thus, both wildlife policy and urban planning, if bereft of this "love, respect, and admiration for the land," are perhaps for Leopold not only flawed, but also potentially baleful, leading to the continued destruction of the planet. The inclusion of both compassion and admiration into an environmental ethic is singular. It creates not only a realignment of nature and the human but also a profoundly different interrelationship grounded upon ecological interdependency and a moral disposition of love, respect, and admiration. This paradigm shift Leopold inaugurates is as much about transforming philosophical understandings of the human subject as it is about traversing the traditional town–country divide.

Thomas Berry: From Biotic Community to Communal Intersubjectivity

Certain philosophical and cosmological implications of Aldo Leopold's ethic have been picked up and placed in a universal context by cultural historian and Roman Catholic priest Thomas Berry. Upon his retirement from Fordham University, Berry established in 1970 the Riverdale Centre for religious research in New York, and became chief architect of the "new cosmology," which addresses current ecological challenges by exploring the role of the human within the larger unfolding of the universe. He views the human as deeply enmeshed not only in the biotic community, but also within the universe itself. For him, the Enlightenment subject is broadened via increased ecological awareness and recent discoveries concerning the mysteries of an unfolding, dynamic universe, confirming by his lights that we dwell not only in a terrestrial biotic community of interrelationships but also within a cosmic communion of intersubjectivities. Berry thus provides innovative directions for ontology, cosmology, and the place of the human within an increasingly urbanized landscape.

With his emphasis on the community-based aspect of life, as well as a profound sense of beauty and the need for admiration of the natural world, Berry views our present ecological moment as a distinctive geological juncture, the closing of the Cenozoic period and the beginning of an as yet unnamed period:

> What is happening in our times is not just another historical transition or simply another cultural change. The devastation of the planet that we are bringing about is negating some hundreds of millions, even billions, of years of past development on the earth. This is a most momentous period of change, a change unparalleled in the four and a half billion years of earth history.[20]

To help nourish the cultural and psychic energy needed to respond to such seismic changes, Berry advocates a deepened awareness of the awesome beauty of the natural world, from a mountain meadow blanketed with flowers to a star-strewn summer sky. Deeply influenced by Jesuit paleontologist and theologian Pierre Teilhard de Chardin, Berry claims that there is a psychic-spiritual dimension to all reality, and that the emerging, expanding universe holds a place for human consciousness as one locus in which the universe, in a sense, reflects upon itself. Building on Leopold's notion of the dying wolf's "green fire" and the mountain "thinking," Berry represents a call away from a commoditized worldview of consumerism and an invitation into a deeper communion, an intersubjectivity, with all of creation. For him, the universe is indeed a "communion of subjects" to be in deep relationship with, rather than a "collection of objects" to be bought, sold, used, and discarded.[21]

For Berry, the stakes are high: "The human community and the natural world will go into the future as a single sacred community or we will both perish in the desert."[22]

Like Leopold, Berry sees the severe limitations of human efforts to manage or control nature. Yet he also sees human inclinations and spontaneities as part of nature, leading to a nuanced understating of the human vocation:

What we need, what we are ultimately groping toward, is the sensitivity required to understand and respond to the psychic energies deep in the very structure of reality itself. Our knowledge and control of the environment is not absolute knowledge or absolute control. It is a cooperative understanding and response to forces ... if responded to properly with our new knowledge and new competencies, these forces will find their integral expression in the ... new ecological age. To assist in bringing this about is the present task of the human community.[23]

Community, Communion, and Cosmology: Implications for the Natural City

As I have briefly outlined, the overcoming of the divide between rural and urban has been a perduring task for much of Western history, but, beginning with modern industrialization and continuing through our present ecological moment, has been offering new insights and opportunities for addressing this dichotomy. The natural city concept is one such approach.

The thought of Leopold and Berry represents, in a sense, an epistemological shift in dealing with both urban and environmental concerns. Just as the Cartesian self-reflective subject framed the early modern period, and the Kantian subject and its inability to perceive absolute knowledge marked part of the Enlightenment, Leopold, Berry, and the environmental movement represent the human as the biotic or cosmological subject, pointing towards a new ontology spurred by our current ecological moment.

Whereas the modern subject is reflected in modern cities built as glorious edifices to the achievements of captains of industry and masters of nature, and the postmodern subject speaks of a protean self constantly remaking its identity and its environment in new and creative ways, Leopold and Berry are speaking of something different: a biotic and cosmic subject. This subject brings wolves and mountains, meadows and stars into a context of multiple subjectivities along with that of the human, providing perhaps a new epistemological pathway into the problem of urban sustainability.

Their insights, by positing a more integrative and humble role for the human, and by probing a deeper understanding of the nature of biotic community and cosmic communion in a collective intersubjectivity with all matter, offer the prospect of the city itself as a new aperture onto the cosmos. Cities are indeed biotic communities, whether they are recognized as such or not, and perhaps constitute a fundamental modality by which we as humans connect with the cosmos. Leopold's land ethic, therefore, is not just for wilderness areas and national parks, but for densely urban sites as well. Just as gravity applies beyond the edges of a city, so too does the biotic community extend beyond designated wilderness areas.

While the idea of a natural city retains a utopian dimension, it also, in light of our present ecological moment, perhaps offers a new critical interface, one that places certain avenues of analysis, including biotic and cosmological analysis, into conversation. As the work of McHarg, Mumford, Spirn, and even the new urbanists intimates, but perhaps does not fully articulate, if urban planning is to remain vital, it must move away from a human-centred, or "anthropotic," orientation, if you will, where green architecture, more parks, and energy-efficient buildings are merely enhancements for the prime inhabitants, i.e., the humans. In contrast, in a "biotic" orientation, the reigning urban ethic is one that privileges the integrity, beauty, and stability of the urban community, in communion with all the subjects that dwell within and beyond city limits.

Just as, for Leopold, the human is "plain member and citizen" of the biotic community, for Berry, the universe is primary, and the human secondary, to the unfolding of creation. When certain philosophical and geographical constructs striving for sustainability, however well meaning, continue to place the human at the centre of both the city and the cosmos, they run the risk of furthering the ultimately self-defeating and death-dealing role of the human as master and conqueror.

Moreover, we run the risk of diminishing our capacity not only to cultivate a love, respect, and admiration for the land, as Leopold urges, but also to develop a sense of awe and joyful celebration when we gaze upon the night sky, or witness the delight of a child running down a grassy hill. By continuing to choose an "anthropotic" rather than a biotic and cosmic perspective, do we risk losing a sense of love, respect, and admiration for the land and for each other? Psychologist and *Tikkun* magazine founder Michael Lerner reflects upon this prospect in his influential book *The Politics of Meaning: Restoring Hope and Possibility in an Age of Cynicism* (1996), wherein he delineates the "destructive ways in which people find meaning" amid the alienation and loneliness of "market societies." To counter such alienation, Lerner proposes shifting society's dominant discourse "from one of selfishness and cynicism to one of idealism and caring"—engaging in a political project to create societies that support "love and intimacy, friendship and community, ethical sensitivity and spiritual awareness" while encouraging people "to relate to the world and to one another in awe and joy."[24]

Lerner's "progressive politics of meaning" is in part a pragmatic, political expression of Leopold's affective ethic and Berry's call to cosmic wonderment. All three thinkers, in a sense, view our ecological and social challenges not simply as serious impediments, but as unique opportunities to develop deeper, more loving, more joyful, and ultimately more life-yielding personal, societal, ecological, and even cosmological relationships.

In reflecting on our present moment, and the choices it places in front of the human community as a whole, Berry invites the human community to what he calls the "great work" of our time: the task of "befriending," rather than besieging, the Earth.

> All indications suggest that we are, in a sense, a chosen group, a chosen generation … We did not ask to be here at this time … some of the prophets, when asked to undertake certain missions, said, "Don't choose me. That's too much for me." God says, "You are going anyway." We are not asked whether we wish to live at this particular time. We are here. The inescapable is before us.[25]

As the challenges of climate change, global poverty, and rapid urbanization deepen, the project of envisioning sustainable urban settlements becomes increasingly compelling. As I have attempted to show, the environmental movement has engendered a tremendous array of fruitful reflection on ecologically fertile ways in which humans can live in urban community, and the sundry roles humans can adopt in such a quest: gardener (Mumford and Spirn), steward (McHarg), or town builder (Calthorpe).[26]

With the challenging ontological and cosmological implications of Leopold and Berry's thought, persons involved in urban planning and environmental concerns are invited to view the human community as members as well as plain, self-reflecting citizens of both the biotic and cosmic communities. They are encouraged to regard themselves as human agents amid a variety of non-human subjects, induced to move with humility, respect, love, awe, and admiration in a participatory, non-masterly role with the rest of creation. It is a daunting yet bracing challenge to bring such a role to the visioning and building of the natural city, but this remains one of the most pressing and promising tasks of our time.

The Ethics of Organic Farming

D
o organic farms, and the organic food industry in general, represent a distinctive social and environmental approach to agriculture? Do they incorporate a unique set of ecological and spiritual values, or merely reflect, on a smaller scale, the same dog-eat-dog, "survival of the fittest" approach of their behemoth agribusiness cousins?

These are questions that will be seeded at the annual Guelph Organics Conference (www.guelphorganicconf.ca), one of the largest such gatherings in North America. There, CEOs of multi-million-dollar organic food companies will share food and reflection with small-scale local organic farmers in a harvesting of concerns and ideas, as the organic food business, once perceived as a hippie-esque pastime for "granola-crunching" bohemians, has grown into a burgeoning multi-billion-dollar industry.

Among those providing a uniquely spiritual flavour to these conversations will be Rev. James Profit, SJ, executive director of the Ignatius Jesuit Centre of Guelph and founder of the Jesuit Ecology Project, which sponsors community supported agriculture, trains young organic farmers, helps restore old growth forest, and blends pesticide-free soil with Christian spirituality to raise both crops and awareness around the spiritual values inherent in farming and food.

Profit, with a hat trick of degrees in agriculture, sociology, and theology, is a long-time member of the Guelph Organics Conference, and has long pondered the spiritual, ecological, and social justice implications of organic agriculture.

In his essay *Connecting with the Earth: Experiencing the Sacred*, Profit notes that spiritual connection with nature does not just happen "down on the farm," but can be nourished even on concrete sidewalks.

"We as a human community can prayerfully spend time with trees, with a compost heap, with the beauty of creation in our own local environment. Even in an inner city, we can experience the life-giving beauty of God expressed by a weed in the crack of a sidewalk. When we experience the Earth as holy ... our actions may change from control and destruction of the Earth, to living in respect for and communion with the Earth."

Profit is part of a larger movement of religious voices worldwide, especially women religious (known as "green nuns"), who see organic farming as a way of building community, promoting spiritual and physical well-being, and expressing respect for the sacred dimension of creation. One of the lighthouses in this field is Sister Miriam Therese MacGillis, a Catholic nun whose Genesis Farm in Pennsylvania has become a mecca for people of faith seeking to root their love of the Earth and dedication to organic farming within a larger spiritual framework.

For Sister Miriam, organic agriculture springs from a sense of deep interconnection with both the Earth and the cosmos. As she observes in one interview: "We're beginning to realize now that the self is an expression of the deeper Earth self, and the even deeper Universe self. ... The feelings of communion, union with the whole ... are no longer just the idealistic notions of poetic insight. ... We know that in our very genes we are connected to the whole. ... When we begin to identify with the whole physical being of the planet, then we can see the necessity of enhancing and conserving the integrity of the whole natural world. ... Without air, water, soil, vegetation, there's no human life. ... The Earth literally is our body."

By placing agriculture within a larger sense of interconnection with a sacred understanding of creation, both Profit and MacGillis are hoeing a row for organic agriculture that leads away from a profit-driven, chemically based, highly competitive, and ecologically destructive agribusiness model. For them, organic farming is not about "survival of the fittest," but about the flourishing of all within a sacred Earth community. Such an approach can yield healthy harvests for us all.

Option for the Poor
and Option for the Earth:
Toward a Sustainable Solidarity[1]

O n December 3, 1984, at five past midnight, tons of noxious gas from Union Carbide's pesticide plant spewed into the city of Bhopal, India, forming a deadly, enveloping fog. Thousands of women, children, men, parents, and grandparents, died agonizing deaths that night—approximately 3800 according to Union Carbide. About 160,000 were treated within 24 hours in the local hospital, gasping for air, their eyes burning, their throats singed with poison gas, all in wrenching pain. Over 8,000 persons, according to local doctors, perished within the next week. In addition, thousands of domesticated animals, migratory birds, and countless wildlife also perished. It remains the worst industrial accident in history.[2]

If this were the end of the story, it would be sufficient tragedy for a lifetime. Yet the horror continues. Over two decades later, the people of Bhopal are still dying from the effects of the Union Carbide disaster, drinking the contaminated water, eating fish from Bhopal's picturesque but now toxic lakes, and remaining exposed to deadly chemicals that have yet to be cleaned up. Deformed and stillborn children are a commonplace in Bhopal, and visitors note few households without someone acutely ill or dying. Some estimate the fatality toll now lies between 16,000 and 30,000, with more than 500,000 inhabitants "injured for life" by the toxic release.[3] Recent medical studies even suggest long-term genetic effects from the gas leaks. Both the Indian government and Dow Chemical, who later bought Union Carbide, consider the matter closed, having achieved a $470 million cash settlement in May 1989.

Welcomed to Bhopal in 1968, the Union Carbide pesticide plant was part of the "Green Revolution," an initiative to help India and other "developing" nations achieve agricultural independence through industrial agricultural scientific advances. Framed within a developmentalist approach to economic progress, as marked by the President John F. Kennedy's Alliance for Progress and the UN Decade for Development, such initiatives were heralded as vehicles for initiative, self-reliance, and economic prosperity for "underdeveloped nations" of the South. Yet, as in Bhopal, so many of these stratagems have become baleful chimeras of deepening poverty and ecological destruction.

Bhopal is but a notorious example of the deepening suffering that certain development agendas have rendered in nations of the South, where promises of prosperity often yield economic and ecological despair for many generations to come. Bhopal is thus a fitting starting point for a consideration of the nexus among poverty, social justice, and environmental despoliation.

Liberation theology, utilizing the social sciences and attempting to read the Bible through "the prisms of the poor," brought an important critique to this developmentalist agenda. By adopting a "preferential option for the poor," liberation theologians were able to identify both the economic bias toward the affluent and the failed promises of prosperity ensuing from developmentalist designs. In this chapter, I will explore how the option for the poor represents: a) a perduring challenge to environmental studies, particularly the notion of "sustainable development"; b) a foundational critique of the notion of "modernity"; and c) a guiding cairn on the path of integrating issues of social justice and ecological sustainability.

The preferential option for the poor, as enunciated by Latin American liberation theologians and later elaborated in ecclesial, theological, and philosophical praxis and reflection, is a foundational concept. In other words, it is a core, rather than peripheral, precept for religious reflection, and can also be one I believe for environmental studies. As one who toils both in the area of religious studies and environmental studies, I wish here to propose that the option for the poor is perhaps one of the most fertile and perduring grounds in which both religious and environmental studies might sink and extend their roots.

Option for the Poor: What Is It?

In order to "opt" for the poor, one must be "non-poor." In other words, one must be in a privileged position to choose a stance of solidarity; after all, one cannot "opt" for what one already is. In this sense, the option for the poor, as originally understood, is an opportunity for engaged compassion of the economically and socially privileged with the economically and socially marginalized. Irish theologian Donal Dorr explains the concept this way:

> An "option for the poor", in the sense in which it is intended here, means a series of choices, personal or communal, made by individuals, by communities, or even by corporate entities such as a religious congregation ... It is a choice to disentangle themselves from servicing the interest of those at the "top" of society and to begin instead to come in to solidarity with those at or near the bottom.[4]

Not surprisingly, one of the most succinct definitions of the preferential option for the poor is provided by Peruvian theologian and pastor Gustavo Gutiérrez, "the founding father," if you will, of the theology of liberation. Gutiérrez breaks down the phrase to component parts: poverty and option.

Poverty, he notes, while consisting of social, economic, and political deprivation, ultimately signifies "death, unfair death, the premature death of the poor; physical death."[5] He writes:

> In the last analysis, the poverty that is lived in Latin America means a situation of premature and unjust death, from hunger and illness or from the repressive methods used by those who are defending their privileges. Besides physical death there is

cultural death from "the devaluation of races and cultures and from the refusal to recognize the full dignity of women ..."[6]

Gutiérrez notes that anthropologists like to say that culture is life: "if you scorn the culture, you scorn life."[7] Moreover, cultural death often marches arm-in-arm with physical death. "That is why," Gutiérrez continues, "in Christian communities in Latin America, we speak often of the 'God of Life' and we reject the opposite: physical and cultural death as well as other manifestations of selfishness and sin."[8]

What is meant by "the poor"? Gutiérrez notes that the poor are the insignificant, those with no ecclesial or societal heft. He writes:

> The poor person is the one who must wait a week to see a doctor. A poor person is one who has no social clout to change the situation. The poor person is the insignificant one who has no economic clout, who belongs to a spurned race, and who has been culturally marginalized. The poor are socially insignificant, except before God.[9]

Gutiérrez provides a compelling eyewitness account of the insignificance of the poor. Participating in the funeral of Archbishop Oscar Romero in San Salvador in 1980, Gutiérrez notes that about 40 persons were killed as shots and explosions shattered the celebration in the cathedral plaza. He observes:

> We know very well Oscar Romero's name because he was an Archbishop, a great man ... But we do not know the names of these 40 people who died in order to see Romero one last time. Beside me, in the cathedral, I saw five dead women, another severely wounded ... We do not know the names of these people because they are poor just as much in life as in death ... They remain anonymous."[10]

In his groundbreaking study, *Teología de la liberación, Perspectivas* (English translation: *A Theology of Liberation: History, Politics, and Salvation*), Gutiérrez developed a compelling notion of liberation with three interrelated, interdependent dimensions:

1) the hope of poor and oppressed persons to achieve economic, social, cultural, and political liberation;

2) the historical reality of poor persons taking the reins of their own destinies and experiencing their agency as historical subjects; and

3) the emancipation, through Jesus Christ, from the bondage of sin.[11]

For Gutiérrez, liberation is a result of what was, in the 1960s, a new political consciousness in Latin America. "Liberation," he noted, "means shaking off the yoke of economic, social, political, and cultural domination to which we have been submitted."[12]

In delineating the features of this domination, Gutiérrez and other liberation theologians sought reading assistance from social scientists, especially those who both articulated and critiqued developmentalist economic theory.

Noting how international development projects represented a profound and powerful social, economic, cultural, psychological, and even ontological and spiritual agenda, Gutiérrez critiqued key tenets of developmentalist theory, as espoused by such prominent developmentalist theorists as Walt W. Rostow, Alex Inkeles, David McClelland, and Talcott Parsons. He noted how such theorists claimed that societies progressed from pre-literate to modern market economies in stages,[13] and that people of underdeveloped nations had to be involved in projects of political maturation to become "modern" persons, whose traits included a developed sense of punctuality, a more serious interest in efficiency, and a propensity to view the world as calculable.[14] Some claimed that self-reliance and an "achievement orientation" were essential characteristics of the modern person, arguing that if certain underdeveloped nations could be "infected" with "n Ach" (the need for achievement), an entrepreneurial zip would begin to spur economic development.[15] Others, espousing an evolutionary approach like Rostow, suggested that the economics of the First World represented the apogee of the evolutionary process, and underdeveloped nations must be helped on their road to develop *just like* the developed nations.[16]

In all the above designs, the development process was seen as universally applicable, regardless of social, cultural, religious, or ecological context. The developmentalist approach suggested that if a state were to merely create a set of conditions, follow a carefully proscribed developmentalist agenda (and just "add water"), a nation could almost automatically achieve "development."

Yet, the historical reality failed to follow the theoretical script. As became strikingly evident by the end of the 1960s, the harvest of this agenda was increasingly grim. Ten years of developmentalist projects and Green Revolution agriculture and industrialization had yielded not the bright promise of prosperity, but trade imbalances, escalating debt, higher infant mortality, lower life expectancy, and a yawning gap between rich and poor.[17]

In short, the developmentalist dream was becoming a nightmare. Moreover, the environmental front fared little better than the socio-economic one: increasing deforestation, urban industrial pollution, and soil and water contamination from chemical-based agriculture were but a few of development's legacies in nations of the South. Significantly, the developmentalist theoreticians had not only failed to take into account local social, political, economic, and cultural contexts in the regions they sought to improve, they also neglected on the whole to consider their ecological contexts, and viewed nature largely as a neutral backdrop on which to paint their master plans of modernization—providing limitless resources and receptacles for waste.

Building on the core-periphery model of Andre Gunder Frank,[18] who argued that underdevelopment in Latin America was a direct consequence of world capitalist development, with the core exploiting the periphery, liberation theologians and philosophers increasingly viewed development and underdevelopment as Siamese twins rather than distant relatives. In other words, you can't have one without the other. Nations do not evolve out of this system into the bracing dawn of abundance and economic independence, but are rather locked into a world system, as social theorist Immanuel Wallerstein would argue, of exploitative, dependent economic relationships.[19]

Development leads to dependence—a situation that the plurality of Latin Americans found themselves by the mid-1960s. Development, for Gutiérrez, only finds its true meaning in the more universal, profound, and radical perspective of *liberation*, which emphasizes the conflictual aspect of economic, social, and political processes.[20] Gutiérrez, in rejecting developmentalism, which had been offered as a balm for the impoverished of Latin America, sought a different term, one that would capture the hopes and aspirations of persons at the bottom and speak to the conflictual nature of society. He chose the term liberation in part as an antidote to development.

Rather than an abstract and ahistorical agenda imposed from above, the notion of liberation, generated by those locked in dependence, takes into account society's political, social, and economic struggles, and represents more accurately, Gutiérrez argues, the aspirations of those on the underside of history.

Gutiérrez, however, also had a strong theological rationale for adopting the notion of liberation. Just as he rejected developmentalist economics, so too did he renounce developmentalist theology. Referring to the "theology" of development, Gutiérrez observes that the mode of theological reflection remains unchanged:

> The error of development … is not a questioning of a type of intelligence of faith; it is not theological reflection in the context of the liberation process; it is not critical reflection from and on the historical praxis of liberation, from and on faith as liberation praxis. To theologize thus will require a change of perspective.[21]

For Gutiérrez, the change in perspective is encapsulated in the term "liberation."

Moreover, the poverty identified by Latin American liberationist thought in the 1960s continues into the present under the banner of globalization, as exiled Argentinean liberation philosopher Enrique Dussel contends:

> Above all, the *reality* out of which such a [liberation] philosophy emerged is today more pressing than ever before in

its continuous and maddening spiral of underdevelopment: the misery, the poverty, the exploitation of the oppressed of the global periphery (in Latin America, Africa, or Asia), of the dominated classes, of the marginalized, of the "poor" in the "center," and the African-Americans, Hispanics, Turks, and others, to whom we would have to add women as sexual objects, the "useless" aged gathered in misery or in asylums, the exploited and drugged up youth, the silenced popular and national cultures and all the "wretched of the earth," as Franz Fanon put it, who wait and struggle for their liberation.[22]

In opting for the poor, a liberationist perspective asks *why* people are poor—a key and unsettling query which helped prompt Gutiérrez and others to look at social scientific systems of development and underdevelopment. The poor are not poor because it is God's will, it was argued, but because of structural injustices; they are not underdeveloped persons; rather, they are fully developed persons who are exploited by unjust economic, social, and spiritual oppression.

For Gutiérrez, while "sin" is always a personal and free act, it is also the rupture of friendship between God and humanity and between ourselves and others. It thus has a profoundly social dimension in the liberationist gaze, for such personal sin leads to unjust social political and economic structures. Hence, building on the social gospel theology of Walter Rauschenbusch and others, liberation theologians spoke in terms of "social" or "structural" sin,[23] concepts affirmed and explored in subsequent magisterial documents.

When applied to the realm of environmental studies, such queries prompt one to ask: Why is there such devastating soil erosion, air pollution, ozone depletion, acid rain, toxic waste sites, and species extinction? Is it simply "God's will" that we are destroying the Earth, the natural consequence of human progress, or does it pertain to social and political "sin," owing to certain economic, political, and cultural systems? The option for the poor compels environmentalists to connect the processes that dehumanize persons to those that denude landscapes. Is there a connection between clear-cut societies in Darfur and clear-cut forests in British Columbia? Moreover, an option for the poor begs the question: Why are aboriginal cultures being destroyed in the Amazon along with the rainforest ecosystem in which they dwell? Is there a connection between opting for the poor and opting for the Earth?[24]

Option for the Poor: A Challenge to "Sustainable Development"

As intimated, one area where the option for the poor has particular significance surrounds the notion of "sustainable development." This term was a key feature of the "global agenda for change," addressed to the UN General Assembly by the World Commission on Environment and Development in 1987. Headed by Gro Harlem Bruntland, Norway's first woman prime minister, the Commission, surveying ecological and socio-economic devastation around the world, articulated the idea of "sustainable development," defined as "meeting the needs of the present without compromising the ability of future generations to meet their own needs."[25]

In many ways the notion of sustainable development is an advance over previous forms of economic progress. It takes into account the need to plan for and think about future generations, and begins to equate social and economic progress with the state of the world's eco-systems. The Bruntland Report, as the Commission's findings became known, argued that the "ability to anticipate and prevent environmental damage will require that the ecological dimension of policy be considered at the same time as the economic, trade, energy, agricultural, and other dimensions."[26] For those exposed to articulations of the option for the poor, however, the notion of sustainable development is lined with dire warning labels.[27]

The idea of sustainable development, despite its advances, appears to eschew the political and economic critiques of development, such as dependency theory, that characterizes much of the liberationist critique from nations of the South. If, as Andre Gunder Frank maintains, one does not have development without underdevelopment, then arguably one does not have sustainable development without "unsustainable underdevelopment." The fact that the nations of the North have not even achieved sustainable development, and are now trying to help prescribe sustainable plans for nations of the South, breeds more than a little skepticism in the non-industrialized world. Add to this that the United States, the world's second-largest emitter of greenhouse gases, continues to refuse to commit to a post-Kyoto framework for limiting greenhouse gas emissions, and such skepticism deepens.

The option for the poor suggests that the poor and marginalized of the world not only be taken into account as new economic and ecological stratagems are devised, but they must be prioritized. Without this prioritization, environmental strategy that produces new forms of marginalization for the poor and for endangered and impoverished ecosystems may result.

The Social Affairs Commission of the Canadian Conference of Catholic Bishops expressed this point forcefully in their controversial 1983 statement on Canada's economic recession:

> The need and rights of the poor, the marginalized and the oppressed are given special attention in God's Plan for Creation. Throughout his ministry Jesus repeatedly identified with the plight of the poor and the outcasts of society (e.g., Ph. 2:6-8; Lk. 6:20-21). He also took a critical attitude towards the accumulation of wealth and power that comes through the exploitation of others (e.g., Lk. 16: 13-15; 12: 16-21; Mk. 4: 19). This has become known as "the preferential option for the poor" in the scriptures. In a given economic order, the needs of the poor take priority over the wants of the rich ... This does not mean simply handouts for the poor. It calls instead for an equitable redistribution of wealth and power among peoples and regions ...[28]

Moreover, the bishops aver that the poor and marginalized must be included in any decision-making process, or economic (or environmental) strategies that will affect their lives, or attempt to improve their condition:

As subjects of creation, all peoples have rights to self-determination, to define their own future and to participate effectively
in decisions affecting their lives ... This is essential if working
people, the poor and the marginalized are going to exercise
their rights to be subjects of their own history ... In effect, the
participation of the marginalized takes precedence over an
order that excludes them.[29]

Adopting an Option for the Poor in Environmental Initiatives

This option for the poor can also be used to enhance and critique
seemingly sanguine environmental campaigns, such as habitat and
wildlife conservation projects. Unless poor persons are consulted
and prioritized in such policy deliberations, one will have misguided
environmental initiatives, such as Project Tiger, according to Indian
environmental scholar Ramachandra Guha. Guha argues such a
project is reflective of a U.S. deep ecological perspective that privileges
"biocentrism" or "wilderness preservation" over "anthropocentrism"
or socioeconomic concerns.

While wilderness preservation might be contextually appropri-
ate for U.S. society given its distinctive demographics and settlement
history, it is inappropriate for India, he claims, with its longstanding
human settlement and dense population in which agrarian communities have achieved a "finely balanced" relationship with their natural
environments. He argues that Project Tiger, a series of conservation
parks hailed internationally as a success, was made possible only by
displacing existing villages and their inhabitants. Prompted by ex-
hunters of India's declining feudal elite in concert with the World
Wildlife Fund and the International Union for the Conservation of
Nature and Natural Resources, the project sought to transplant a U.S.
style park system onto the Indian landscape. Claiming that the resulting
parks are geared toward affluent tourists, Guha claims that the needs
of the local population were not taken into account.

Consequently, more pressing environmental problems facing
India's poor, such as water erosion, fuel, air, and water pollution, have
been eschewed. Such an import of an American wilderness ethic, Guha

maintains, ultimately masks the two most pressing ecological dilemmas facing the world: overconsumption by industrialized nations of the North and urban elites within nations of the South, and growing militarization, manifested both in regional conflicts and the threat of nuclear annihilation.[30]

Just as Gutiérrez and other liberation theologians sounded a tocsin of concern over the developmentalist agenda, so do Guha and other environmentalists of the South issue a warning against recent sustainable developmentalist stratagems. In both cases, the top-down approach of the empowered nations avoids an appreciation of, or a consultation with, the lived experience and social, economic, cultural, political context of the marginalized, which in many cases is the majority of their intended beneficiaries. In addition, in both cases, the poor involved in the stratagems are not only excluded, but also often further disenfranchised.

Just as the three aspects notion of liberation—economic, historical, and spiritual—have to be taken together in addressing the needs of impoverished persons, so too with economics, politics, and ecology in dealing with impoverished ecosystems. In a sense, they form a "seamless garment" out of which the tapestry of sustainability must be sewn. And unless the stitching of that garment includes the hands and hopes of the marginalized poor, the ultimate fruit of that labour may well be used to further diminish the poor and the ecosystems within which they dwell. In this sense, the Greek notion of *oikos*, household, from which derive the words economy and ecology, has relevance; no household is sustainable in which the children die of starvation or malnourishment, the pets perish from poisons, and the plants die from neglect or wanton destruction.

Option for the Poor and a Critique of Modernity: The Emergence of a Social Ecology

The option for the poor, combined with a contextualized concern for destroyed ecosystems, has led liberation theologians such as Leonardo Boff and Ivone Gebara of Brazil to adopt a "social ecology," as distinct from a wilderness ecology, in a manner similar to

Ramachandra Guha. Such an ecology sees a correlation between the "cry of the poor" and the "cry of the earth," and pays special attention to marginalized peoples, such as the aboriginal groups in the Amazon, whose traditional lifeways are razed along with the rainforest in pursuing commercial interests of ranching, mining, timber, as well as other enterprises. For Boff, the ecological crisis points to a fundamental crisis of the modern world, erected upon an exploitative economic pattern of development and underdevelopment, whose ultimate harvest is death:

> We have never seen death on such a scale today caused by unemployment, low wages, disease, and violence. Dozens of still surviving indigenous peoples are rapidly disappearing. In this way, we shall lose forever forms of humanity of which we have great need.[31]

As Boff has pointed out, the preferential option for the poor and oppressed in liberation theology leads to a broader critique of the modern project, the modern self, and our role as humans.

Enrique Dussel has been at the forefront of the critique to which Boff refers and succinctly articulates the liberationist critique of modernity:

> We were conscious of being the "other face" of modernity. Modernity was born in 1492 with the centrality of Europe; eurocentrism originated when Europe was able to dominate the Arab world, which had been the center of the known world up to the 15th century. The "I," which begins with the "I conquer" of Hernan Cortes or Pizarro, which in fact precedes the Cartesian *ego cogito* by about a century, produces Indian genocide, African slavery, and Asian colonial wars. The majority of today's humanity (the South) is the other face of modernity; it is neither pre- nor anti- nor post-modern, nor can this South "end" or "realize" such a modernity.[32]

Dussel argues that the notion of the "modern" self did not begin with René Descartes's celebrated insight, "I think, therefore I am," but rather with the New World conquistador's apprehension, "I conquer, therefore I am." In vanquishing the great Incan and Aztec empires, the European, Dussel argues, discovered himself and herself as "modern," rather than primitive, and therefore "superior." In this sense, conquest of the other was inherent to the notion of modernity.

Dussel, highlighting an insight of Gutiérrez, notes that, whereas the European political theologians deal with the oppressed but modern human subject, the liberation theologians deal with the oppressed "non-person" of the South.[33] Dussel, after describing what a liberationist vantage critiques, outlines what it envisions:

> We propose a Philosophy of Liberation of the Other that is beyond the horizon of the economic-political-hegemonic world (fratricide), of the eurocentric communication community (filicide), of the phallic eroticism which castrates women (uxoricide) and last but not least, the subject which uses nature as an exploitable mediation for the valorization of the value of capital (ecocide).[34]

Here Dussel stretches his liberationist philosophy to include the biosphere, and links it with other forms of death. In this, his ecology is one that is simultaneously social, economic, political, and ontological, suggesting that within the fabric of the environmental crisis, the threads of social, economic, political, gendered, and cultural oppression are vibrantly woven.

Liberation theologians such as Dussel, Boff, and Gebara are attempting to construct an "alternative and integral modernity."[35] They are fashioning a social ecology that delineates a social justice framework, adopts a preferential option for the poor, and seeks a holistic integration of these approaches within an appreciation of the Earth's ecosystems.

Constructive Ecological Responses to the Option for the Poor

An option for the poor can be seen in a variety of ecological initiatives around the world, both faith-based and secular. The social ecology advocated by Guha and Boff, as well as Indian environmentalist

Vandana Shiva, is reflected in the hundreds of social/environmental groups that have been formed in the last two decades throughout nations of the South, with over 500 emerging in Latin America alone, most of which are located in cities and all of which adopt a "social" ecology that see poverty as a primary environmental issue.[36]

One tangible expression of these movements is the World Social Forums that have gathered in Porto Alegre, Brazil and elsewhere within the global South since 2001, which bring together thousands of environmental, social, political, cultural, and religious groups from around the world, especially impoverished nations. As theologian Lee Cormie observes, despite the wide diversity of these gatherings, there are nonetheless significant points of important convergence around ethical and ecological concerns.[37]

Moreover, the World Council of Churches (WCC), with its Justice, Peace, and Integrity of Creation initiative, was one of the first international Christian organizations to integrate environmental concerns within its justice and peace agenda. In addition, with its important work on climate change under the pioneering direction of Dr. David Hallman, it demonstrated the effects of climate change on the most poor and vulnerable around the world. In his sense, the option for the poor continues to animate its environmental ministries.

Throughout North America and in various countries throughout the world, sundry religious orders are engaging in "ecoministries." Roman Catholic women's religious congregations in particular have for the last three decades taken the environmental challenge seriously. These groups have rewritten their chapters and reworked their lands to include community-supported agriculture, using energy efficient and non-polluting technologies such as solar heating, and have turned manicured lawns into wild lands, and preserved seeds and restored polluted or degraded landscapes. Just as women's orders were among the first to institutionally embrace and integrate the teachings of Vatican II (1962 – 1965), so too have they been among the first to incorporate environmental concerns systematically and institutionally in their ministries. Known as "green nuns," these women have consistently adopted both a preferential option for the poor as well as an interest in the wonders and mystery of creation, particularly inspired by the important "new cosmology" of "geologian" Thomas Berry and mathematical cosmologies of Brian Swimme.[38]

"Ecological debt" groups of Southern nations have also done dynamic work synthesizing an option for the poor with environmental destruction through the lens of international debt. Citing the historical conquest and colonization of their lands, the appropriation and patenting of their various seeds and ancestral knowledge, the continuing ecological destruction of their nations to fuel foreign debt payments, they note that the nations of the North owe an "ecological debt" to nations of the South which has not been acknowledged, let alone repaid.[39]

The International Jubilee movement also reflected a compelling nexus between a concern of the earth and concern for the poor. Building on both the biblical notions of Sabbath and Jubilee, where after seven and forty-nine years one forgives debts, lets the land lie fallow, and releases slaves, Jubilee groups around the world campaigned on these fronts marking the fifty years after the Bretton-Woods agreement set up the International Monetary Fund and the World Bank. In the Canadian Ecumenical Jubilee Initiative, for example, the three-year campaign focused on canceling the debt of some of the poorest nations of Africa, ending economic slavery around the world, and advancing aboriginal rights and addressing ecological destruction. An option for the poor infused all of the Jubilee efforts.[40]

Many other areas of religious and environmental work could also be cited, such as environmental racism, which highlights the targeting of toxic waste sites in poorer neighborhoods of colour, and ecofeminism, which notes the dual oppression of women and nature. Increasingly, then, the option for the poor is permeating environmental analysis.

Importantly, the option for the poor not only animated justice, peace, and solidarity groups within the churches during the 1970s and 1980s, it also arguably led to the church institutional infrastructure through which environmental concerns are now being expressed, as evinced by the WCC's efforts, as well as the linking of ecological work to justice and peace ministries. The option for the poor, in other words, helped form the institutional "hook" on which the churches would begin to hang ecological concerns. And, through sharing the same ecclesial foothold, tenuous as it may be in certain cases, the mutual interests and interrelation of these two critical initiatives—social justice and ecology—are being explored and expanded.

Conclusion

In sum, then, the option for the poor proffers at least four key insights for the environmental movement:

1) The impoverishment of the human is embedded in, not parallel to, ecological destruction; in other words, both are expressions of the same process. Poverty, in this sense, is grounded in "unequal ecologies."[41]

2) The poor, as non-persons, are not only eclipsed in a metaphysical, philosophical sense (modernity), but are also often excluded environmentally, or literally displaced, in conversations and projects of ecological sustainability.

3) Environmental devastation emerges out of (and contributes to) the unequal conditions of power that characterize the world; moreover, such power differentials are not random, but are rather historical and structural.

4) Cosmological shifts to a new appreciation of and regard for the Earth have to be integrated within a social analysis of how the global-political economy continues to generate ecologically grounded poverty. Ecological cosmologies are thus challenged to embrace political and economic structures, recognizing their origins in cultural ideas and practices.

As the Bhopal tragedy reveals, schemes for development are often more disastrous than fruitful. In viewing Bhopal from the perspective of the poor, certain hidden realities are rendered visible: an abundance of cheap labour, a dubious location of a factory near concentrated and indigent populations as well as a critical watershed, a political system with weak environmental and labor standards; in short, a population and an ecosystem vulnerable in almost all categories. In Bhopal, economic poverty and loss of jobs that affect the residents' livelihood do not only ruin lives; residents now experience their "livinghood" jeopardized as their entire ecosystem is tinctured. Even if the citizens of Bhopal now were to get additional jobs or higher wages, their environment is perhaps permanently contaminated. As Bhopal grimly manifests, the option for the poor is not just about economics and politics, it is fundamentally about the environment as well. In Bhopal, marginalization henceforth occurs along economic, political, and ecological trajectories.

In helping articulate a critique of the developmentalist agenda, the option for the poor provides an important, sobering antidote to the promises of economic and political prosperity emanating from Northern nations, as well as a caveat specifically to sustainable development stratagems. The option for the poor also raises a perturbing and still largely undigested critique of the modern project itself, out of which most of our academic and environmental studies programs and initiatives spring. This stance forces privileged environmentalists to look at their own ideological and economic biases, and take seriously the participation of endangered human communities, such as Amazonian tribal peoples, as well as endangered species, in their proposals. This option has also given rise, as suggested, to several challenging and dynamic movements that are trying to integrate issues of poverty and marginalization within an ecological framework, in hopes that the underside of future well-intentioned social and ecological projects might be discerned before their fulsome potential is fully expressed.

On Sacrifice, Spirituality, and Silver Linings

D id you ever think of giving up your car?

When I posed this question to my wife several years ago, she rolled her eyes and the bubbles above her head flashed the words "Ridiculous!" "Impossible!" "Recycling and composting are fine, dear," I heard her thoughts missile toward me, "but this is going way too far."

I felt like Galileo proposing a heliocentric universe to Pope Urban VIII. Suddenly, I was questioning a sacred tradition. After all, this was the way the world had been since the ancient Greeks. Wasn't it Heraclitus who said that to be fully human one needed locomotion, preferably in a Lexus? I suddenly was asking with Prufrock, "Do I dare disturb the Universe?"

After a cup of tea, though, some calmness settled onto the conversation. She and I were able to discuss pros and cons of not renewing the lease on our car now that we were living in the city. On the plus side, we knew that we would save some money—some estimates claim an annual savings of $7000—and it would be environmentally beneficial. According to Pollution Probe, an average lightweight car in Canada annually spews 4480 kilograms of carbon monoxide, 200 kilograms of carbon dioxide, and a noxious soup of other gases.

On the downside, we knew that it would be an inconvenience. We would be dependent on public transit, shopping would be more labour intensive, and if we had an emergency with our young son, we would have to rely on friends, cab, or ambulance.

After several months and many tea-ridden colloquies, however, my wife joined me in the heliocentric universe. We gave up the car. (During our first "car-less" weekend, my wife rented a car. It sat in the driveway.)

Interestingly, we both viewed the prospect as primarily a sacrifice. But a funny thing happened on the way to a car-challenged lifestyle. We gradually became aware of unforeseen benefits, silver linings that "came dropping slow" into our horizon of awareness.

First, we noticed less stress in our lives. Instead of waiting till the last minute to get somewhere, plopping in the car, snaking our way through traffic snarls and snarling motorists, and bickering about what would have been the best route to take, we found our travel was more relaxed on public transit. I also wasn't burdened with a low-grade anxiety about getting a ticket, or being towed, or changing the oil, or driving through lousy weather.

Secondly, we found on the streetcar or subway that we could talk together as a family. Our streetcar time became a family story time. After dropping off our son, my wife and I would then often walk downtown to work together. Car-less living had led to enhanced family bonding.

Thirdly, we noticed a marked decrease in impulse buying. We were much less likely to go out in -20 degree weather or a rain-soaked evening to get a video or a dessert or some other non-essential without a car. Also, we were reluctant to buy anything larger than a loaf of bread without serious strategizing.

Less stress. Increased family bonding. Diminished consumerism. We had not counted on these when we decided to relinquish our vehicle. These were for us spiritual as well as material benefits.

As Canada ponders the sacrifices and costs of a Kyoto accord, perhaps we might view striving for societal sustainability as not just a matter of sacrifice. This isn't about everyone giving up one's car; it's about discerning how we are to relate to this new ecological moment. Sometimes fundamental changes make room in your life for new and fine things to happen. It's not just about sacrifice, but about making a space for a novel and possibly enhanced way of life. It may also hold hidden harvests for the spiritual and material well-being, not only of our families and nation, but of our larger household, the Earth.

Christmas Invites Us to Make
Peace on Earth a Reality

In the 1947 celluloid gem, *Miracle on 34th Street*, a Macy's department store Santa, played delightfully by Edmund Gwenn, tries to lead a jaded 7-year-old girl, Susie Walker (Natalie Wood), to the shores of the imagination.

"You've heard of the British nation. And the French nation," Kris Kringle explains. "Well, this is the Imagi-nation." With such a wondrous metaphor, a hitherto unexplored world of dreams, hope, and joy breaks open for a soul-pinched child. A space for faith, which the film defines as "believing in things when common sense tells you not to," is opened, through which the daughter and her love-scarred mother plunge into a new life.

For many of us in North America, particularly in a post–9/11 milieu, we share a sensibility with the cynical Susie of the film. We find it difficult to imagine peace in a landscape saturated by a "war on terror."

While we have little trouble getting into the gift-giving dimension of the season, which dovetails nicely with an overblown consumer culture, we seem to have a much greater difficulty embracing one of the chief invitations of Christmas: "Peace on Earth, and goodwill toward all."

Christmas, as proclaimed by heralds in the night skies over Bethlehem, is in a sense an invitation to think about things differently, especially about peace. It can create a moment, a space, in which we can break out of "business as usual" and reimagine what is possible.

Since the attacks of 9/11, however, the prospect of peace, both in terms of policy and our cultural imagination, has largely been erased from our collective zeitgeist. From the bloody, unconscionable U.S. invasion and continued occupation of Iraq to the perduring war in Afghanistan, war-making, rather than peace-building, seems to get top billing in both our policy and mindset. And too often, our television programs and films accent the need for extreme measures, including the acceptability of torture, to protect national security in a seemingly permanent war.

As cultural theorist Edward Said (1935–2003), author of the acclaimed work *Orientalism* (1979), suggests, taking away the ability to imagine what is possible is a form of tyranny, a tyranny of the imagination.

Jesus of Nazareth interestingly also faced a tyranny of the imagination. Born in first-century Palestine, a land under the bloody heel of Roman occupation, he imagined a community where lepers, beggars, prostitutes, tax collectors, and Roman centurions could all share in the fruits of creation. Amid mass political crucifixions and deep religious taboos, he bespoke a kingdom based not on armies and military superpower crackdowns, but on love, kindness, truth, and justice. He confronted the political and cultural tyrants of his own time and courageously declared that a peaceful world is possible.

The Christmas story of a child born in a stable suggests that not only was there "no room in the inn," but in fact there was no room in the mainstream culture of the time for the birth of such a radical vision of love and civil serenity. Christmas thus represents both a timelessness and a "time out of time," a moment of peace to give us the breathing room to imagine a world of peace.

Pundits will, of course, say peace is impossible in today's world. And they have a bevy of current events on their side. We are indeed facing wars, economic disparity, ecological destruction, and deep enmity on so many fronts. Yet for peace to be possible, one doesn't always have to strive for the impossible. Sometimes it is enough merely to achieve a "coalition of the unlikely"—people, circumstances, and events that against the odds begin to coalesce around a common purpose.

The Christmas event epitomizes the unlikely. How likely was it that, for the Christian worldview, God's son would be born, not among the wealthy and powerful, but among barn animals in a manger? Yet, interestingly enough, despite its improbability, such a birth was discerned by the Magi who entered into this realm of the unlikely by charting a star and travelling great distances in order to experience the Christmas gift of peace.

There are all kinds of unlikely things that come together at Christmas—I recently stumbled on a YouTube clip in which the erstwhile gender-bending glam rocker David Bowie teams up with the swing-era, cardigan-clad crooner patriarch Bing Crosby in a reworked "Little Drummer Boy," which asks in compelling musical fashion, "Peace on Earth: Can it be?" With grace, good humour and mutual respect, this unlikely duo sings of the pressing need to envision a peaceful world and to journey this Christmas to the free world of the imagination.

Christmas welcomes us to such unlikely harmonies. In "singing along," we help break the "tyranny of the impossible."

Questions to Ponder
and Exercises to Consider

1. In "Christmas Invites Us to Make Peace on Earth a Reality," Scharper speaks of the present "tyranny of the imagination" as an oppression over our creativity that binds us from imagining a world of peace. We can see this same tyranny at play when it comes to imagining different ways of doing weddings, deciding not to own a car, choosing to eat organic foods, and even becoming vegetarian or vegan in our consumption of food. Take a moment to consider all the ways we are inhibited in our mainstream culture from radically re-envisioning our world. How might we overcome the tyranny that oppresses our creativity in these instances?

2. In "Option for the Poor and Option for the Earth," Scharper applies his political theology of the environmental approach to articulate a critique of the developmentalist agenda. He shows how the option for the poor "provides an important, sobering antidote to the promises of economic and political prosperity emanating from Northern nations, as well as a caveat specifically to sustainable development stratagems." Through such an approach, he is able to reveal how schemes for development are often more disastrous than fruitful and that marginalization "occurs along economic, political, and ecological trajectories." Now it's your turn. Applying what you now understand about the political theology of the environment approach, how would you rate current "development" projects in your country or abroad, whether led by a government or by non-governmental agencies?

Take your time with this one. If you are not up-to-date on national or international development projects, start reading newspapers (the business section is a good place to read about mining "development" projects), government websites or literature from non-governmental agencies: examine one project from the perspectives of those struggling for dignity, freedom from sexism and economic oppression, as well as ecological sustainability for the entire planet. What are your findings?

3. Here's an exercise you can do every time you walk through your neighbourhood, village, or city. In "From Community to Communion," Scharper challenges all persons involved in urban planning and environmental concerns to "view the human community as members as well as plain, self-reflecting citizens of both the biotic and cosmic communities." As you walk past familiar sites in your town, think of how you might redesign things to develop deeper, more joyful, and ultimately more life-yielding personal, societal, ecological and even cosmological relationships. Why do you suppose some life-giving elements are presently missing from your community?

4. In "From Community to Communion," Scharper talks about a comfort zone economy. He quotes Leopold as saying, "We all strive for safety, prosperity, comfort, long life, and dullness," concluding that "too much safety seems to yield only danger in the long run." What do you suppose Leopold means by this? Do you think we have arrived at a point in our culture where we have become too safe? Why or why not?

5. Again, in "From Community to Communion," Scharper underlines that it's not enough to see ourselves only as plain citizens of the biotic community, but of the cosmic community as well. This is a lesson learned from Thomas Berry, who "advocates a deepened awareness of the awesome beauty of the natural world, from a mountain meadow blanketed with flowers to a star-strewn summer sky." Why is seeing ourselves as being part of the cosmos as well as the biotic community so important? In what ways does it make a difference to how we transform ourselves as humans?

Conclusion

From Sustainable Development to Sustainable Liberation: Toward an Anthropo-harmonic Ethic

Unless we see Earth as our primary ethical touchstone,
we will be as water skeeters on the surface of the deepest—
and most deeply troubled—ethical ponds.

Stephen Bede Scharper

Throughout the three sections of this book, we have been encouraged to participate with our whole being in Stephen Scharper's analysis and reflection on our global ecological crisis and deepening poverty. We might feel anger, sadness, or fear brought on by what we have been doing to the planet and to one another. And so we should, since the sense of wonder, awe, joy, and love we experience when we are in intimate relation with one another and our planet have been, from the beginning of time, the sources of the physic energy we need to live in harmony with all creation.

Having taken a long, critical look in the mirror, we realize the urgency in which we need to redeem ourselves from our pathological quest to consume and deface the natural world. The process will require the nurturing of an imaginative, creative space so that we can begin to address the most crucial question humankind faces today: What is our role as humans on Earth?

A number of thoughtful Christian ethicists and social scientists of our time have accepted this challenge and, as we have seen in the three sections of this book, have suggested various metaphors of the human as "steward," or "gardener," in order to navigate the ethically turbulent waters of anthropocentrism. To truly liberate ourselves—and in concrete ways—from our present destructive ways of being, though, Scharper stresses that we must rid ourselves once and for all of any notion that we are masters or conquerors of our world, and begin to see ourselves as "just plain members and citizens" of the biotic community.

But Scharper's political theology of the environment approach does not allow him to stop there.

He reminds us that we cannot overlook the fact that poverty is often grounded in "unequal ecologies" and that a majority of human beings are not even granted the status of citizen, let alone "plain citizen." If the impoverishment of the human is embedded in, and not parallel to, ecological destruction, how might we reimagine the entire human community on Earth?

This is the promise of Scharper's anthropo-harmonic ethic. It offers us a unique and valuable way of redeeming the time. This last chapter will investigate this new ethic by addressing three main questions: What are its features? How does it function? And what steps can we take toward living out an anthropo-harmonic way of being human?

The responses will come in the form of a conversation Stephen and I had on this very issue, with my questions appearing in italics. The goal here is not to present a definitive and fully worked-out code for human behaviour, but to present a vision and process for reimagining a new way of being human. The conclusion, and indeed the book, will end with some closing thoughts Stephen has on his anthropo-harmonic ethic for the reader to consider.

Simon Appolloni

Describing an Anthropo-harmonic Ethic

With anthropo-harmonism, you suggest—and are the first to do so, as far as I am aware—that we retain the "anthropo," since this affirms us as human citizens participating in the world and—given the lessons learned from the mirror check you discussed earlier—affirms our potency as a species. But the "centrism" disappears in order to underline that we are no longer focal; however, your ethic nevertheless leaves us with our powerful self-reflective consciousness, our freedom, and, hence, our importance. In what manner are you suggesting we are powerful yet should no longer be "central" to our deliberations?

This question gets to a number of dimensions that are a little onion-like in terms of their layers. First of all, anthropo-harmonism is something that comes from a reflection on anthropocentrism, bio-centrism, and then cosmocentrism, in terms of looking at some of the environmental discourse on what should be "central" to our delibera-tions. But within this conversation, the role of the human is sometimes overlooked, exaggerated, or undervalued, and so anthropo-harmonism is a way to say that we will never be able to shed our human skin—our *anthropos*, in other words. We will never be able to see the world the way a blue whale does or the way a snail darter does; we will always be looking at reality through human eyes, and so the "anthropo" has to remain.

However, what we do not have to do is see ourselves as lord, mas-ter, conqueror, and centre of all that is. And so that's why "anthropo-harmonism" is suggested: while we don't drop the anthropo, as we will always read reality through a human lens, we can drop our hubris that suggests we are the centre of both the biotic and the cosmic journey. Instead, we accept that we're in a "radical intersubjectivity" with all of creation.

You spoke of the radical co-penetration of the human and non-human in "From Community to Communion." Would this be the same thing as radical intersubjectivity? In what way are we in radical intersubjectivity with the non-human? And what bearing does it have in the formation of your anthropo-harmonic ethic?

Yes, radical intersubjectivity could be looked upon as the co-penetration of the human and non-human, as well as among humans. And this bears much upon the anthropo-harmonic ethic. The reality is that we are only one species among many species, and that we, too, are dependent on clean air, clean water, non-pesticide–laden food and clean soil. You could say that "no subject is an island," as it were, because intersubjectivity is a fundamental reality of all existence. In fact, we have this radical intersubjectivity with creation, whether we acknowledge it or not. Furthermore, one can be fully human only when the individual and communal elements of being human are integrated in such a way that they sustain all creation. The achievement of this integration is "harmony"—not only among humans, but also between humans and the rest of the biotic community.

Anthropo-harmonism, then, recognizes two important streams of ethical thinking:

- that humans are dependent on one another—which is why anthropo-harmonism affirms the social justice paradigm put forth by ecofeminism and liberation theology; and

- that humans are dependent on the natural world and the natural world is, in some sense, dependent on humanity.

Think of it as a "dialectical contingency" among humans and between humanity and the rest of creation.

You are suggesting, then, that our interdependency should be looked upon as a dialectical contingency. How is this so? Could you explain how dialectical contingency functions, specifically in regard to the human–non-human relationship?

Lately I have become more aware of the "agency" of non-human nature. By agency, I mean the ability that non-human nature has to exert influence over us. So while we can accurately speak about the agency humans have over nature, we must also speak about the agency non-human nature has over us. This is perhaps why my reflections seem a little different from those of Leonardo Boff, Rosemary Radford Ruether, and even Thomas Berry, to a certain extent: because I think

I've really been challenged to listen to aboriginal voices of interrelationship. This is not to say these other thinkers haven't, but for me, I think, this is key: our radical intersubjectivity implies that nature is not a backdrop to us, or simply an inspiration for us as gardeners, or stewards. Consider how we're in radical shared dependency with the air, fire, earth, water, and the other elements. There is a back-and-forth interaction going on. This is the dialectical contingency: we know that we affect them, but these elements also affect us, and in a kind of radical and often unnoticed, unseen way.

Let me give you an example. When Danny Beaton, a Mohawk activist, says, "Brother fire is helping me," he really means what he is saying. The fire is not just an element that has no connectivity to him, or just some physical relation that keeps him warm; it interacts with him. My wife, Hilary, and I have experienced the agency of fire ourselves. We have noticed, for instance, that some of our best conversations, our most profound and far-reaching exchanges, have occurred near the fire and by the waters of Georgian Bay, Ontario.

Over time, we began to realize that this is not an accident. It's not like we were just inspired by the aura and ambience of the elements. No, the fire and the water were working on us: we were having our conversation because the fire was participating; we were having this conversation because we were participating with the water. Both elements were affecting us at the neurological level as well as the psychic-spiritual level. The fire and water changed us while we changed them. Our relationship with them, then, is not a static thing; it's more like a dance.

And it need not be just water and fire. Aldo Leopold hinted at such dialectical contingency in *The Sand County Almanac*, where he talks about environmental history. He notes that the history of settlement in the United States was affected by the vegetation. Leopold describes how in certain cases, our settlement patterns have been largely determined by Kentucky bluegrass: where it grows and where it doesn't. Thus, different grasses and grains helped shape human history. We often ignore this fact. And we often overlook its implications on our ethics: that our relationship with the natural world is not simply biological but moral.

How the Anthropo-harmonic Ethic Functions

What you describe as anthropo-harmonism places much import on our interdependency and interconnection with one another, and between the human and the non-human, which certainly, at the intuitive level, feels right. I imagine many humans would feel the same way. Yet we don't see many humans living in a way that recognizes this dialectical contingency. I have trouble, therefore, seeing how anthropo-harmonism might work. How might your ethic address this seeming chasm between what we know we ought *to do and our* actually doing *it?*

As we have seen in the previous chapters, anthropo-harmonism insists that feelings of awe and reverence for the universe play a crucial role in forming a lasting integration between humans and non-humans. We can make ourselves more knowledgeable, change all our laws, fashion new policies, and even design cutting-edge sustainable technologies, but none of these will take hold until we change our relationship with creation. In developing a "love, respect, and admiration" for the biotic community to which we belong, we begin to see ourselves as being just "plain members and citizens." This deeper communion with the natural world helps us to see ourselves, as Thomas Berry liked to put it, as a "communion of subjects" rather than a "collection of objects."

But there is a second and important outgrowth from this. As I stated above, we have a radical intersubjectivity with creation whether we acknowledge it or not. By acknowledging that we are only one species among many, and that we, too, are dependent on clean air, water, soil, and so on, we acknowledge our own vulnerability and, hence, a need for humility. I suggest that it is precisely the *absence* of humility and—by extension—the presence of an excessive ambition and self-confidence that allows us to think that we can pollute the air, pollute the water, pollute the soil and still live happy, healthy lives. It's pathological when you think of it, because it denies our radical intersubjectivity and the constant interactive state we are in with non-human nature.

I often give my students the example of inviting friends over for a barbecue: "Hey, come on over for a barbecue. I'll get the drinks," you say. Then you come around with a gasoline can and start filling up the glasses. Suddenly, everyone present exclaims disgust and incredulity at your actions and calls on you to stop. You say, "It's OK! I cleaned out the container; it's lemonade!" This might seem like a bizarre example, but when you think of it, that's what we are doing with our lakes: "Let's throw in all our effluents, our oil, salt from the winter, and chemicals that we do not test for; we'll clean it and serve it to you." It's pathological.

The notion of "climate prosperity" is another good example of this pathology. The idea behind climate prosperity is that some of us might do well with the arrival of global warming because of the longer growing season here in Canada and the northern United States. Yet, as I will explain, this notion is ludicrous and sinfully unjust.

A number of years ago, I was at a think tank in Guelph, Ontario, where politicians, journalists, academics, and scientists gathered to reflect on climate change. A freelance journalist who was present raised the idea of climate prosperity without using the term, implying, "Hey, won't this be good for us in the North?" The journalist was interested in knowing how we could "manage" climate change so we can benefit from it. One scientist who had been quiet all weekend immediately spoke up: "There is no scientific evidence that there can be any benefit from climate change; in fact, it will likely lead to chaos in terms of flooding, insect infestations, and absolute irregularity in weather patterns. In short, there is no scientific evidence that this will be helpful at all."

The scientist's rejoinder didn't seem to deter this journalist from talking about climate change as a good thing. We have to ask ourselves, however, why people are increasingly finding southern varieties of black widow spiders in homes in Connecticut when previously this was not the case: our weather is so mild due to climate change that such creatures are moving northward. If we do not protect the biotic community, it will snap right back and bite us, literally, in the form of a black widow spider.

What's more, the journalist did not realize that climate prosperity for some—those of us in Northern climates—ultimately means climate disaster for many. There is a direct correlation between our driving cars and the rising seawaters flooding lowland farmlands in

Bangladesh. This is why this term is so fulsome: it denies the radical intersubjectivity we have with others and all creation. And that's the myth of climate prosperity, that somehow you can build a wall between yourself and the social and ecological ills of the Earth.

I understand how a love, respect, and admiration for creation, accompanied by a healthy dose of humility, could indeed lead to our privileging the integrity, beauty and stability of the entire biotic community. What I am still unsure about, given our new position as just plain members and citizens of the biotic community, is who gets to define beauty? Integrity? Stability? What do you suppose a raccoon would say on each issue? A stream?

I think that is an excellent question. It's one that requires a deep kind of layering of thought and response. First of all, I think it's important to note that the idea of privileging the integrity, beauty and stability of the entire biotic community comes from Leopold, and that he is writing in the 1940s. He suggests—as does Rachel Carson later on—that a democratic tradition is the most viable method for preserving the integrity, beauty and stability of a biotic community. Why? Because it gives voice to people who are being sprayed by pesticides, or it gives voice to people who are in the toxic dumpsite zones of Love Canal; it gives voice to those who live in black neighbourhoods and have asthma because they are inhaling the incinerator fallout.

So, for me, the question of who gets to define the integrity, beauty, and stability of a biotic community is entrenched in a democratic process that has to be expanded. It's not a perfect process, by any means. Winston Churchill once said that democracy was the worst form of government, except for all the others. So for me, anthropo-harmonism can be done only within a democratic framework.

With this democratic process in mind, we can now address the question of who gets to define what's what. Thomas Berry would talk about environmental impact statements (EIS) in the United States—documents describing the positive and negative environmental effects from proposed actions—as a beginning of this democratic process. It is where humans begin to ask the permission of the land to develop.

This process didn't exist until recently. It's almost as if we are saying to the land, "Hi, I want to build a parking lot; what do you think?"

Now, environmental assessments are not foolproof by any means. However, with them, there is a legal moment when we are asking the permission of the land: Can the land sustain this? Can the biotic community weather our development? Or does it need to be protected from human development? The development of wilderness preservation areas, restrictions of wetland development, and the protection of endangered species areas are all, in a sense, attempts to involve the biotic community in the democratic determination of beauty, integrity, and stability.

Obviously we're anthropo, so we will never know what the river "wants" and we will never know what the raccoon "thinks." But when we see raccoons going into our garbage in downtown Toronto, for instance, given all the unbelievable and unbridled sprawl that has occurred within the city in the last 20 years, we can certainly ask whether he or she is here in our compost bin because we have clear-cut areas north of the city, areas that were farm fields not 30 years ago. For the same reasons, we are forcing the coyotes to come into our backyards because we have destroyed the integrity, beauty, and stability of *their* biotic community. We didn't ask permission of the land to sprawl Toronto all over it.

While such a democratic process makes sense to those of us living in North America (where democracy is practised), you are suggesting an inter-species democracy where a certain status of citizenship is granted to all within the biotic community. I'm curious to understand how the anthropo-harmonic approach might deal with conflicting wants and desires among species in the community.

There are two things about conflict to note here. The first deals with liberation, the principle of liberation theology that views the human as a principal actor in his or her lifeway. Liberation is explosive; there is no getting around this. It involves breaking unjust structures, social stratification, taking the history of the aboriginals seriously, taking sides with those who are marginalized, as well as the radical in-breaking of the divine. Liberation theologians, as Jon Sobrino discussed in "The Ecological Crisis," have taken a hard line to keep their liberationist positions from being diluted: there must be a preferential option for the poor.

Thomas Berry has taken an equally hard line by saying the Earth is primary! In both cases of solidarity with the poor or with the Earth, social conflict is inevitable. In "Option for the Poor and Option for the Earth: Toward a Sustainable Solidarity," we saw two main groups represented by conflicting worldviews: one that seeks "sustainable development," which I have shown is not possible, as it is exploitative, and another that is searching for "sustainable liberation." Unlike development, which is linear in its process and invariably managed from above, liberation comes from many directions but is a bottom-up process in its thrust. Liberation, therefore, suggests irruption. This is why some refer to liberation as the "irruption of the poor." I suggest that with regard to all we have done to damage and exploit the Earth, we can now refer to the "irruption of the Earth."

Second, when the disagreement occurs between the human and non-human, we have to consider what Thomas Berry says about the role of analogous and imaginative thinking. He maintains that in discussing the rights of animals and the rights of rivers, too often we get stuck because we are so literalist and fundamentalist in our thinking. Instead, if we were to think imaginatively and analogously, we would see that animals, rivers, and humans all have intrinsic rights, except that the rights are not the same.

Philosopher and theologian Michael Vertin once put it in a simple and creative way. He said, "God is good; pizza is good; God is not pizza. The analogy is in the good." Similarly, Berry would say humans have rights and birds have rights, but they are not the same rights. Each has rights specific to its species. So human rights are not the same as bird rights. An analogous thinker can say birds are not humans. The analogy is in the rights, not in the bird or human. Birds are not humans, and it would be wrong to give birds human rights.

It is for this reason that the anthropo-harmonic ethic requires an imaginative space where we can employ our imagination and imagery. Conflicts among species need not necessarily be seen as conflicts when we approach the situation with analogous and imaginative thinking.

Steps Toward Living out an Anthropo-harmonic Ethic

While it is clear now why we need to fall in love with the Earth as a key point of departure for your anthropo-harmonic ethic, it is not altogether clear how we might begin to do—or at least continue to nurture—this love. What might you say to someone who asks you, "How do I fall in love with the Earth?"

I find that there are three parts to the process of falling in love. There is the *practice of love*, the *preparation for love*, and the *doing of love*. It might help to explain what I mean by these by way of story.

I'm up in Bruce Peninsula, Ontario, in a provincial nature reserve, a wilderness area where there is a bird observatory and, consequently, many birding experts. I met one of them who taught me how to do the Screech Owl call; this is a difficult call to do. I mean, a lot of them are hard. But this one requires that you put your head back, put a certain amount of saliva in there, and have air go over that saliva so that there is a gurgle. It took me two weeks to learn that call. So I'm doing this for two months up on the Bruce Peninsula, never once successful in calling up a Screech Owl.

One morning, around 5:45 a.m., months later in downtown Toronto in Cedarvale Ravine, I'm taking a walk and practising my Screech Owl call. And I hear a response. I'm in disbelief, thinking, this can't be right. I do it again and I hear the call. I do it again and the Screech Owl lands on a branch right above me. And I continue to call and he or she responds. Then another Screech Owl comes across the pathway and lands in another tree off the path. So there's a trialogue going on: me, the owl above me, and the one across the way.

Soon they start making sounds I've never heard, which is fascinating. These aren't the sounds I was taught; they are other kinds of cackling and calling. These birds are conversing in a way that is so beyond my ability to imitate that I'm just listening. Finally, after 10 or 12 minutes, they're still going on, and I'm thinking, "Hey, I've got to keep moving, get my son up, get his breakfast ready … you guys knock yourself out, I've got to go; sorry." Everything in me wants to stay and hear this conversation, but I have to get moving as they continue to dialogue.

This episode harkens back to an experience I had as a child when I learned how to do the Mourning Dove call. One morning, in the front yard of a neighbour's house where there was a patch of trees, I had a conversation with a Mourning Dove for what seemed like 30 minutes. I was absolutely enthralled. I thought, "Oh my gosh, I have no idea what I'm saying, but we are having a conversation!" This was my first real experience of this kind of call and echo with non-human nature, aside from pets. I kept thinking how cool this was: we can respond to them and they can respond to us. It was so mysterious, but also exciting. And it was a very important experience for me in nature.

That call became a signal in my neighbourhood, as a couple of my friends also knew how to do it. It became our signal in all our adventures. When I went out to play, I wouldn't need to call them on the phone, I'd just need to make the sound and, if I heard a response, we were together. So what started as a way of communicating with the Mourning Dove became a kind of code among friends.

Since part of our identity as boys was spending time in nature, catching frogs, tramping through the woods, trumping over streams, flying over rivers, you know, testing ourselves in the wild, that call became so important: we felt a romantic affinity with aboriginals in the sense that they would use such bird calls to communicate with each other. And so, for us, this was our kind of aboriginal communication system.

When developers came and started chewing out these beautiful forests and fields that we played in, we felt they were violating what was our special place. I mean, this was almost like an old growth forest that became so much a part of our identity. I couldn't say for sure, but some of the nearby oak trees had to be about 200 years old. Yet the developers filled in the ponds where we went swimming and where the muskrats lived, and built an office building. They tore out fields where we ran and put in tennis courts. For me and for a couple of my friends in particular, we felt that we were experiencing something radically wrong; it was such a violation of what we held dear.

Often, we would show our displeasure with this situation. We always had the sense that we knew this terrain better than the inter-lopers did. So with our bird-call system, we were able to communicate among ourselves so they wouldn't see us on the land, upon which, ironically, they considered us trespassers. What was interesting was that our call, matched with the call of the birds, brought us in a kind of solidarity with them, for both the bird's habitat and our habitat was being destroyed. We used the same communication as the Mourning Dove, whose trees were being destroyed, the same trees that were our playground.

Here's the thing, though. For both the Screech Owl call and the Mourning Dove call, it took me weeks to learn those calls. Not everyone in my neighbourhood learned how to do the dove call. Others would try to mimic it and you knew immediately who it was, because only a couple of people in the 'hood knew how to do it. The guys who stuck with it are some of my best friends still, and we still know each other by this call. Often, I will teach my students and young people these calls. Some will stop because they don't get it right away; others keep refining and practising the call until they got it.

Apart from this practice of love, for me the preparation for love was sticking with it, because the communication has to be with the hands and done in a particular way to be authentic. The preparation enabled us to communicate more effectively over time and over a wider range, because you can go very loud with this call and communicate hundreds of yards. Preparation involves much discipline, just like learning to play an instrument. There's a certain authenticity involved that comes through preparation, which doesn't happen overnight.

Finally, there is the doing of love. This is where we experienced the awe, the fun, and the touch, both physical and spiritual, of the natural world. It is also where we experienced sadness and a sense of loss. In fact, the destruction of the habitat hurt so much because we were bound to that land; it was such an organic part of us that when it was destroyed, we saw it as a major violation. Something was cut: we were injured spiritually, injured psychologically, and injured physically when this area was destroyed.

It appears, then, that for an anthropo-harmonic ethic to take effect, the whole person—in body, mind, and spirit—needs to participate in the practice, preparation, and doing of love. It's not just a head thing. Considering how this process brought you in solidarity with the bird, how might it work with the broader creation?

I'm always struck by Gustavo Gutiérrez's pithy comments. He says, "Unless you know the names of a poor person, you are not in solidarity with them." So, unless you know them as Joe, Mary, or Juan, and can converse with them as such, while you might be in intellectual solidarity with them, you are not fully in solidarity with them. I think Gutiérrez's statement has relevance for the Earth: unless you know the names of certain species, learn how to communicate with them, spend time with eco-systems, with rivers, discern the patterns of animals that move across your life course, your ravines, you are not in solidarity.

For Gutiérrez, it's totally a matter of relationship. He always talked about this as pastor in the poor barrios in Lima, Peru. For him, liberation theology is a second act; the first act is solidarity and love with people who are struggling for justice. In fact, he said he never mentioned the term "liberation theology" in his parish in Lima. Being in loving solidarity with people who are struggling to live a decent life is the most important thing; and that came about, for Gutiérrez, by entering into relationship with them. Reflection on it is secondary.

We can say the same for falling in love with the Earth. What's most important with regard to anthropo-harmonism is whether you are in loving relationship and courageous solidarity with the plants, animals, and humans that need you. For me, knowing well a place on Earth is such a mysterious but important dimension of solidarity with the Earth and with each other.

When I am at the Bruce Peninsula, I go to this one place as often as I can and take long walks. I feel as if the trees know who I am because I spend hours there almost every morning walking its trails. I wondered once why I went only to this one spot; there are certainly other places to go. But I felt drawn to this particular place, wanting to get to know this part of the Earth better. I felt I really needed to try and dwell in this place and learn to know it as best I could, to try to imbibe it, absorb it.

It was later that I learned that this place—called Singing Sands because when the wind comes off the lake and over the sand, it makes a hum—was saved from development by a group of citizens. All this shore on Lake Huron was being subdivided for cottages, but a group of people said, "Enough. This has to be preserved!" So, for me there was the human dimension of love and care for that land. It all could have been developed—and almost was, for the plans were there—yet local citizens came together and saved it. The same act of solidarity occurred with my ravine where I go to hear the Screech Owl. That was the main drag for the proposed Spadina Expressway in the 1970s, but urban theorist Jane Jacobs and other concerned citizens saved it.

So hearing the Screech Owl and being in touch with the trees at Singing Sands both have a connection through solidarity and political action that saved a part of nature's lifeway. I think that is one reason why I am drawn to both places: there but for the grace of these concerned individuals would be development, highways, destruction. It was just plain members and citizens who got together and, out of love, respect, and admiration for land (using Leopold's language), tried to protect the integrity, beauty, and stability of those biotic communities. They did this, I suggest, because they knew the land.

And that is the way we become bound in responsibility for the Earth. We must all continue to fight for these lands that are being destroyed; to these people I never met, I am indebted. I often thank them when I walk. I also thank Jane Jacobs, and I thank the people who founded the Federation of Ontario Naturalist preserves and Singing Sands. I feel responsible to continue that legacy.

Closing Thoughts on the Anthropo-harmonic Ethic

In his analysis of the history and development of ethics, religious scholar Houston Smith tells us how ethics originally grew millennia ago out of newly realized necessities to "get along" with people outside their primary group who were encroaching on their land. Something more than local rites, rituals and procedures were needed to avoid the growing discord among humans as they navigated expanding personal encounters. Out of this grew the Golden Rule. With our newly realized necessity to "get along" with the rest of the biotic community, it would seem that both Leopold and Berry are calling for our ethics to evolve anew. Can you comment on this?

Well, I think that this notion of ethics evolving is new to certain people. When I talk to my undergraduate students, for example, we talk about human evolution and they think of biological evolution. They don't necessarily think of ethical evolution. So I often ask them, "Have our ethics evolved and can you give an example of our ethics evolving, even in your lifetime or in the last 50 years?" Some will point to the UN Declaration on Human Rights as a moment of a collective ethical evolution reflecting on the needs of the human family. But some will talk about more simple things: the fact that smoking is no longer allowed in public spaces, recycling is widely practised, and so on. I remind them that 40 years ago, their parents might have tossed garbage on the ground without thinking about it. Today, if their parents can't find recycling receptacles, they feel guilty about discarding their recyclable product into the regular garbage.

For me, a real mensch in this evolution is Aldo Leopold. His reflection is that it's time now to expand our ethics to include the biotic community. He begins with a page out of Greek history where Odysseus, returning from his wars and finding out that a spate of slaves have been unfaithful, has them executed. Leopold notes that in the ethical protocol of the day, Odysseus's actions were not a problem, because slaves were considered property: they had no ethical standing.

Today, we have evolved to a point where we see slavery as unethical and immoral. It took a long evolutionary train to get to that point. But we got there. And now Leopold's point is that we have to look at our relationship of the biotic community as a subject of ethics. Leopold was the first to articulate the need for the biotic community to come under the purview of ethical reflection. That's why he is sometimes called the father of environmental ethics.

Thomas Berry reminds us that our ethics have not kept pace with our power. While we have codes and penalties concerning suicide, homicide, and genocide, we have no prescriptions against geocide. The hope is that the concept of geocide becomes part of an evolutionary approach to a legal as well as an ethical understanding of Earth.

Consider the period after World War II in Nuremberg, following the Holocaust. Humans were able to develop both an ethical and a legal imperative to prosecute Nazi war criminals. Those who obeyed the law but not their conscience, arguing, "I was just following orders," were put to death. Our ethics evolved, and today, with the International Criminal Court in The Hague, we have legal instruments to deal with war criminals and those who perpetuate crimes against humanity.

The examples above point to both an evolution of our ethical theory and an entrenchment of that theory in legal regulations, laws, protocols, and penalties. This is what Berry is talking about when he talks about geocide. We have the legal apparatus to deal with homicide and with genocide; now we need the legal apparatus to deal with geocide. So while it's certainly the evolution of an ethical horizon that we must come to grips with, it is also a legal one.

In one of your writings, not included in this book, you stress, "Unless we see Earth as our primary ethical touchstone, we will be as water skeeters on the surface of the deepest—and most deeply troubled—ethical ponds."[1] So while our ethics and legal codes must evolve, it seems as if there is a grave urgency to do so. Can you elaborate on this?

As you point out in your introduction to this book, now is the time to act, given the kind of ecological destruction we are forcing upon the Earth. Berry would point out often that we as humans are closing down the life systems of the planet. As David Orr says in *What is Education For?* each day we force 40 to 120 or so species into extinction, many of which we haven't identified yet. We're closing down so many species that it's creating a new geological epic or epoch. And as you point out, some geophysicists are proposing that our period of time be called the Anthropocene. This is something Berry had talked about 30 years ago, but it wasn't looked at seriously until recently. Now that hard-nosed scientists—people who are not prone to hyperbole—are talking about the destruction of the Earth, people are listening. Moreover, scientists are confirming that this evolution of ethics is vitally important now: if we do not find an ethical way of preserving those species facing extinction, like water skeeters on a troubled pond, we're in danger of cutting off the supports for life: certainly for humans, and certainly for a quality of life for a majority of humans, that will be sustainable, habitable, and livable.

Is there any last point about your ethic that you would like to discuss?

Yes. This deep sense of intimate interrelationship with all of crea-tion is, in part, why I think the aboriginal recovery is so essential. Part of our modern identity of being lords and masters over creation came with the conquest of the aboriginal peoples in North and South America some 500 years ago. These are peoples who, in large measure, saw their existence bound in dialectical contingency with the Earth, and many still do so today. Part of the modern project, when we con-quered the "New World," involved breaking that relationship with the Earth and denying our dialectical contingency with non-human nature. The work of anthropologist Timothy Ingold has been helpful in understanding how we broke this relationship; I'd like to finish by discussing it briefly.

Through his anthropological reflection of native cultures, he says, "We totally missed the boat! We would look at these aboriginal tribes in Amazon and we would see them talking with trees and birds. And since we were kind people, we would say, 'They are not crazy; it is all metaphorical. They are not really dialoging because then they would be nuts; it's a metaphor, something akin to a play or shadow dance ….'" Ingold explains that we denied the possibility of real communi-cation between human and non-human nature through our modern arrogance. In a condescending, polite, respectful way, we simply put a different gloss on it, to save the aboriginals some dignity.

He stresses, however, "We never entertained the possibility that they were *really* communicating with the trees, and now we realize that maybe they are communicating, that there is perhaps a psychic-spiritual dimension to all living things."

In all my research, I have come to understand that there is something happening between humans and non-humans that we just can't explain, and might never be able to. But we, in our hubris and our anthropocentrism, and our Western cultural dominance, do not entertain that possibility.

I believe we are being called not only to a new understanding of our world but to a new *way* of understanding our world, one that can incorporate the dialectical contingency I spoke of earlier. Certainly, we must incorporate the values of social justice, liberation, and human freedom, but all within a construct that takes non-human nature seriously.

A new way of understanding our world should take seriously an aboriginal relationality with nature. This is not saying that everyone has to go back and live on the land as we did 500 years ago. No, this is a moment of retrieval, redeeming, reflecting, a dialectical swirl of reinterpretation for this time.

And this leads me to a final point about understanding anthropo-harmonism and our dialectical relationship with Earth. Until we deal authentically, humbly, and honestly with aboriginal lifeways, what we have done to the aboriginal peoples, and what they continue to tell us in their traditional teaching, until we take that seriously and have a real truth and reconciliation moment, with all that process entails, I'm afraid that our relationship with the Earth is not going to deepen much further.

The traditional aboriginal lifeways of North America (and elsewhere on the planet) and the agency of the Earth itself have been paved over, literally and figuratively, by our Western mindset, our colonial expansion, and our intellectual trajectories that deny a psychic-spiritual dimension to the universe. So unless we recover our aboriginal understandings, we are, first, not going to treat our aboriginal people as anything but antiques, museum pieces or holdovers from another time; and second, unless we take seriously their worldview of relationality, which speaks in large measure to the agency of nature, we're not going to rekindle our own aboriginal sensibilities, and we're not going to be in relation with the Earth in an anthropo-harmonic way.

As many aboriginal lifeways suggest, what we are called to is not a mere fine-tuning of our reasoned ethical systems. Rather, we are invited to relationship—a relationship with all of creation that involves affection, compassion, celebration, and joy. Ultimately, we are invited not merely to "think better" about how to relate to nature; rather, we are invited to fall in love with the Earth.

Endnotes

Foreword

1   Editorial. "Learning to Live in a Changing Climate." *The Financial Times.* July 2, 2012, 10.

2   Johan Rockstrom et al. "Planetary Boundaries: Exploring the Safe Operating Space for Humanity." *Ecology and Society* 14(2) [2009]: 32. http://www.ecologyandsociety.org/vol14/iss2/art32/ (accessed July 17, 2012).

3   M. Sparke. "Unpacking Economism and Remapping the Terrain of Global Health." In *Global Health Governance: Crisis, Institutions and Political Economy,* ed. Adrian Kay and Owain David Williams. International Political Economy Series (Basingstoke, UK: Palgrave MacMillan, 2009), 131.

4   Fox Searchlight Pictures. 2012. *The Best Exotic Hotel.* See: http://www.foxsearchlight.com/thebestexoticmarigoldhotel/ (accessed July 17, 2012).

Green Dreams: Religious Cosmologies and Environmental Commitments

1   Marina Herrera, "Theoretical Foundations for Multicultural Catechesis." In *Faith and Culture: A Multicultural Catechetical Resource* (Washington, DC: United States Catholic Conference, 1987), 8.

2   For a helpful overview of contemporary scientific analysis of climate change and other signs of ecological concern, see D. B. Conroy and R. L. Peterson, eds., *Earth at Risk: An Environmental Dialogue Between Science and Religion* (Amherst, NY: Humanity Books, 2000). See especially Charles J. Puccia's (2000) article therein.

3   For more information, one may consult the National Religious Partnership for the Environment website at www.nrpe.org/mission.html.

4   Thomas Berry, with T. Clarke, *Befriending the Earth* (Mystic, CT: Twenty-Third Publications, 1991), 7–8.

The Ecological Crisis

1   Peter W. Bakken, Joan Gibb Engel, and J. Ronald Engel, in their assiduously researched survey of Christian Ecojustice Literature, suggest that theologian Joseph Sittler's 1961 address—"Called to Unity"—to the Third Assembly of the World Council of Churches in New Delhi marks the outset of post–World War II attempts to interweave environmental concerns, justice, and Christian faith (see Bakken, Engel, and Engel, *Ecology, Justice, and Christian Faith: A Critical Guide to the Literature* [Westport, CT: Greenwood Press, 1995]). For careful assessments of Sittler's ground-breaking ecological theology, see Steven Bouma-Prediger, *The Greening of Theology: The Ecological Models of Rosemary Radford Ruether, Joseph Sittler and Jürgen Moltmann* (Atlanta, GA: Scholars Press, 1995); and Bruce Heggen, "A Theology for Earth: Nature and Grace in the Thought of Joseph Sittler (Ph.D. diss., Montreal, McGill University, 1995).

2   See Lynn White Jr., "The Historical Roots of Our Ecologic Crisis," *Science* 155 (1967):1203–7.

3   According to the Intergovernmental Panel of Climate Change, global temperatures may rise by 1 to 3.5 degrees Celsius by 2100 owing to fossil-fuel emissions, leading not only to alarming weather patterns, but also to dramatic effects upon plant and animal

ecosystems, including the northward spread of such tropical diseases as yellow fever and malaria.

4   For up-to-date and thorough statistics on environmental issues, see the annual report of the Worldwatch Institute, *State of the World*, edited by Lester Brown.

5   Rachel L. Carson, *The Sea Around Us* (New York: Oxford University Press, 1951).

6   When *The New Yorker* magazine printed pre-publication excerpts from *Silent Spring*, it received menacing legal correspondence from the U.S. chemical firm Velsicol, as did Houghton-Mifflin, Carson's publisher. For a cogent treatment of U.S. corporate attempts to silence *Silent Spring*, see the 1993 PBS video *Rachel Carson's Silent Spring*, part of *The American Experience* documentary series.

7   Rachel Carson, *Silent Spring* (Boston: Houghton Mifflin, 1962), 297.

8   Carson's childhood imagination was fuelled by the nature-study movement, represented by botanists Liberty Hyde Bailey and Anna Botsford Comstock. Comstock's *Handbook of Nature Study* (1911), widely used by elementary school children in North America, taught the fundamental principles of birds, fish, and animals, and sought to instill a love of nature in children. In the case of Carson, it was apparently most successful. For further background on the movement and its influence on Carson, see Linda Lear, *Rachel Carson: Witness for Nature* (New York: Henry Holt, 1998).

9   Max Oelschlaeger, *Caring for Creation: An Ecumenical Approach to the Environmental Crisis* (New Haven, CT: Yale University Press, 1994).

10 Quoted in Thomas Sieger Derr, "Religion's Responsibility for the Ecological Crisis: An Argument Run Amok," in *Worldview* 18 (January 1975):39–45.

11 Stephen B. Scharper, *Redeeming the Time: Toward a Political Theology of the Environment* (New York: Continuum, 1997).

12 Robin Attfield, *The Ethics of Environmental Concern* (New York: Columbia University Press, 1983); Derr, "Religion's Responsibility for the Ecological Crisis"; H. Paul Santmire, *Travail of Nature: The Ambiguous Ecological Promise of Christian Theology* (Philadelphia: Fortress Press, 1995).

13 Douglas John Hall, *Imaging God: Dominion as Stewardship* (Grand Rapids, MI: Eerdmans, 1986).

14 Jürgen Moltmann, *God in Creation: A New Theology of Creation and the Spirit of God* (San Francisco: Harper & Row, 1985).

15 Rosemary Radford Ruether, *Gaia and God: Toward an Ecofeminist Theology of Earth Healing* (San Francisco, HarperCollins, 1992); Sallie McFague, *The Body of God: An Ecological Theology* (Minneapolis, MN: Fortress Press, 1993); Heather Eaton, *Introducing Ecofeminist Theologies*. New York: T&T Clark International, 2005; Vandana Shiva, *Monocultures of the Mind: Perspectives on Biodiversity and Biotechnology* (London, Zed Books, 1993).

16 Leonardo Boff, *Ecology and Liberation: A New Paradigm*, trans. John Cumming (Maryknoll, NY: Orbis Books, 1995); and Ivone Gebara, "Cosmic Theology: Ecofeminism and Panentheism," in *Readings in Ecology and Feminist Theology*, ed. Mary Heather MacKinnon and Moni McIntyre (Kansas City, MO: Sheed and Ward, 1995), 208–13.

17 Thomas Berry, *The Dream of the Earth* (San Francisco: Sierra Club Books, 1988).

18 For a more detailed listing of such groups, see Stephen B. Scharper and Hilary Cunningham, *The Green Bible* (Maryknoll, NY: Orbis Books, 1993), 109–11.

19 Texts of such church statements are included in Drew Christiansen and Walter Grazier, eds., *"And God Saw That It Was Good: Catholic Theology and the Environment* (Washington, DC: United States Catholic Conference, 1996).

20 See the chapters by Virgilio Elizondo and Lee Cormie in *The Twentieth Century: A Theological Perspective*, ed. Gregory Baum (Ottawa, ON: Novalis, 1999).

21 Thomas Berry, *Befriending the Earth: A Theology of Reconciliation Between Humans and the Earth* (Mystic, CT: Twenty-Third Publications, 1991).

22 Boff, *Ecology and Liberation*.

23 Scharper, *Redeeming the Time*.

The Gaia Theory: Implications for a Christian Political Theology of the Environment

1 As Gaia changed from a hypothesis to a theory, it might be helpful to distinguish between the two descriptions. A hypothesis is only a provisional scientific understanding of how particular things work in our universe. A hypothesis can turn into a theory, though, as was the case with the Gaia theory, when it becomes well-substantiated through much testing, observation, and experiments. Consequently, the Gaia theory is now generally accepted by the scientific community. It was in 1988 that the Gaia hypothesis was subjected to its most sustained scientific scrutiny. In March of that year, the American Geophysical Union, the international association of geologists and geochemists, dedicated the entire week of its biannual Chapman conference to Gaia. Leading scientists from around the globe gathered to debate the premise and details of the Lovelock and Margulis findings. This conference marks a turning point when the Gaia hypothesis became increasingly referred to as the Gaia *theory* in scientific circles. See Elisabet Sahtouris, "The Gaia Controversy: A Case for the Earth as Living Planet" in Peter Bunyard and Edward Goldsmith, eds., *Gaia and Evolution: Proceedings of the Second Annual Camelford Conference on the Implications of the Gaia Thesis* (Cornwall, England: Wadebridge Ecological Centre, 1989), 55.

2 Lovelock describes the provenance of the Gaia hypothesis in *Gaia: A New Look at Life on Earth* (New York: Oxford University Press, 1979), 1–24. Though Lovelock first presented the Gaia hypothesis at a 1969 scientific conference at Princeton, he did not publish his idea until 1972 in a letter to *Atmospheric Environment*.

3 Lovelock, *Gaia*, 9.

4 Lynn Margulis and Dorion Sagan, *Microcosmos: Four Billion Years of Evolution from Our Microbial Ancestors* (New York: Summit Books, 1986), 267.

5 Lawrence E. Joseph, *Gaia: The Growth of an Idea* (New York: St. Martin's Press, 1990), 2.

6 Anthony Weston, "Forms of Gaian Ethics," *Environmental Ethics* 9 (Fall 1987):219.

7 Sahtouris, "The Gaia Controversy," 57.

8 Joseph, *Gaia*, 83.

9 Joseph, *Gaia*, 8.

10   Margulis and Sagan, *Microcosmos*, 15.

11   Margulis and Sagan, *Microcosmos*, 15–18.

12   Bunyard and Goldsmith, *Gaia and Evolution*, 7.

13   Bunyard and Goldsmith, *Gaia and Evolution*, 9. Lawrence Joseph, the colourful journalistic chronicler of Gaia, observes that since the 1988 conference, about 100 scientific and technical articles have been written on the Gaia theory. Many of these articles seem less concerned with the verity of the theory than with its leading authors to novel questions and approaches in their respective specializations, some of which challenge the fundamental orientation of their disciplines (Joseph, *Gaia*, 13).

14   Lovelock, *Gaia*, 40–43.

15   Lovelock, *Gaia*, 27–28.

16   Lovelock, *Gaia*, 110.

17   Lovelock, *Gaia*, 112.

18   Lovelock, *Gaia*, 115.

19   Lovelock, *Gaia*, 80, 105.

20   Ironically, it was Lovelock's own research in the Arctic using his important invention, the electron capture detector, that made the discovery of the first "ozone hole" possible. With the ability to detect Freon and other halogenated compounds in the air, this device helped trigger ecological concerns over ozone depletion and ultraviolet radiation–engendered cancers (Lynn Margulis and Dorion Sagan, "Gaia and Philosophy" in Leroy S. Rouner, ed., *On Nature* [Notre Dame, IN: University of Notre Dame Press, 1984], 74).

21   On the ecological sensitivity barometer, Lynn Margulis fared little better than does Lovelock, partially owing to the minuscule role she also ascribes to the human within Gaia. As suggested earlier, because animals are "Johnny-come-latelys" to Gaia, Margulis intimated that animals, including humans, are merely delivery systems or incubators for the microorganisms that really control Gaia's functioning (Margulis and Sagan, "Gaia and Philosophy," 68). Margulis and Sagan claim that Gaia can still be seen primarily as a microbial production and that humans are relegated to "a tiny and unessential part of the Gaian system" (Margulis and Sagan, "Gaia and Philosophy," 71). Not to deny completely a role for the human, Margulis proposes that humanity has the potential to be an anxious "early warning system" for Gaia, detecting how Gaia might be injured by various human activities or other changes. Moreover, we humans might be able to colonize other planets and deflect oncoming asteroids, thereby protecting Gaia. Such a diminutive role, she maintains, should not make us "depressed." Rather, "we should rejoice in the new truths of our essential belonging, our relative unimportance, and our complete dependence upon a biosphere which has always had a life entirely of its own" (Margulis and Sagan, "Gaia and Philosophy," 73).

22   Norman Myers, ed. *Gaia: An Atlas of Planet Management* (London and Garden City, NY: Gaia Books and Doubleday, 1984).

23   Frank Barnaby, ed., *The Gaia Peace Atlas: Survival into the Third Millennium* (London and New York: Gaia Books and Doubleday, 1988).

24   Interestingly, such volumes don't engage or challenge the Gaia hypothesis per se; they
      in effect use it as a springboard to show how humans must tread more respectfully on
      the planet. For a delineation of some of these Gaia-inspired religious and New Age
      developments, see Joseph, *Gaia*, 66–71.

25   For a pragmatic response to Gaia, see Kit Pedler, *The Quest for Gaia* (London: Paladin,
      1991). Pedler argues that the Gaia theory is a new revolutionary force that has been
      unleashed on the world. Technologists, he argues, have made the egregious blunder
      of assuming that nature was passive and neutral, a vast piece of blank paper on which
      they could draw their dreams. Instead, Pedler contends, the life process that surrounds
      us is characterized by an intelligence capable of self-rectification and regulation, an
      insight provided by Lovelock (Pedler, *The Quest for Gaia*, 10). Unlike the Gaia theory
      originators, Pedler ascribes a hefty role to the human in living within Gaia. Pedler
      contends that we must reorient ourselves to live in harmony with Gaia, otherwise we
      face extinction. For Pedler, we are in Gaia. There is no way to extricate ourselves from
      it; we are neither above nor superior to it. He suggests that no sustainable future for
      humanity can be attained unless human concerns are placed second to Gaian concerns.

26   William Irwin Thompson, "Gaia: A Way of Knowing," in David Cayley, ed., *The Age of
      Ecology: The Environment on CBC Radio's Ideas* (Toronto: James Lorimer and Company,
      1991), 168.

27   Thompson, "Gaia," 172–73.

28   Thompson, "Gaia," 182.

29   Anthony Weston, "Forms of Gaian Ethics," *Environmental Ethics* 9 (Fall 1987).

30   Weston, "Forms of Gaian Ethics," 220.

31   Weston, "Forms of Gaian Ethics," 223.

32   Weston, "Forms of Gaian Ethics," 225.

33   Weston, "Forms of Gaian Ethics," 228.

34   Weston, "Forms of Gaian Ethics," 228.

35   Douglas John Hall, "The Integrity of Creation: Biblical and Theological Background
      of the Term." *Reintegrating God's Creation: A Paper for Discussion.* Church and Society
      Documents. September 1987/No. 3 (Geneva: World Council of Churches, Programme
      Unit on Faith and Witness, Sub-unit on Church and Society), 32.

36   Hall, "The Integrity of Creation," 34–36.

37   Rosemary Radford Ruether, *Gaia & God: An Ecofeminist Theology of Earth Healing*
      (San Francisco: HarperCollins, 1992), 5.

38   Ruether, *Gaia & God*, 57.

39   Ruether, *Gaia & God*, 265–72.

Ecofeminism: From Patriarchy to Mutuality

1   *Theology Today* editor Patrick D. Miller insightfully depicts this quest in feminist
      theology. Claiming that a deeply felt resistance to aspects of divine sovereignty within
      feminist theology is not surprising, Miller continues: "The Bible itself sets forth notions
      of husbandly rule over wives and male rule over women and then tells of stories about
      such rule that curl the hair. Perpetuation of ecclesial male domination in hierarchical

modes in the church and elsewhere simply reinforces the conviction of women that notions of sovereignty carry with them patterns of domination that suppress full and mutual responsibility, opportunity, and reward. It is to be expected that out of such encounter with human sovereignty, theologians, female and male, would seek to discover or construct a kind of theology that reveals a God in whose nature and activity mutuality or some other kind of relationship replaces hierarchical control of the world and its creatures and whose imaging is appropriately set by images that are more open, gentle, vulnerable to others, and preserving of freedom in the creation in all its forms" (Patrick D. Miller, "Editorial," *Theology Today* 53, no. 1 [April 1996]:2).

2   Charlene Spretnak, "Critical and Constructive Contributions of Ecofeminism," in *Worldviews and Ecology: Religion, Philosophy, and the Environment*, ed. Mary Evelyn Tucker and John A. Grim (Maryknoll, NY: Orbis Books, 1993), 261.

3   Karen Warren, "The Power and Promise of Ecological Feminism," *Environmental Ethics* 12, no. 3 (Summer 1990):132.

4   Lois K. Daly, "Ecofeminism, Reverence for Life, and Feminist Theological Ethics," in *Liberating Life: Contemporary Approaches to Ecological Theology*, ed. Charles Birch, William Eakin, and Jay B. McDaniel (Maryknoll, NY: Orbis Books 1990), 88–108; Carol J. Adams, ed., *Ecofeminism and the Sacred* (New York: Continuum, 1995).

5   Adams, *Ecofeminism and the Sacred*, 2.

6   Adams, *Ecofeminism and the Sacred*, 2.

7   Marjorie Casebier McCoy, "Feminist Consciousness in Creation: 'Tell Them the World Was Made for Woman, Too,'" in *Cry of the Environment: Rebuilding the Christian Creation Tradition*, ed. Philip N. Joranson and Ken Butigan (Santa Fe: Bear and Co., 1984), 132.

8   Adams, *Ecofeminism and the Sacred*; Spretnak, "Critical and Constructive Contributions of Ecofeminism," 261.

9   For theologian Lois K. Daly, there are four main tenets of ecofeminism: (1) oppression of women and oppression of nature are interrelated; (2) this interrelationship must be probed to overcome these dual oppressions; (3) feminist analysis must include ecological insights; and (4) any suggested ecological solutions must entail a feminist perspective (Daly, "Ecofeminism, Reverence for Life, and Feminist Theological Ethics," 88–90).

10   Rosemary Radford Ruether, "Ecofeminism and Theology," in *Ecotheology: Voices from South to North*, ed. David G. Hallman (Maryknoll, NY: Orbis Books, 1994), 199.

11   Adams, *Ecofeminism and the Sacred*, 3.

12   Adams, *Ecofeminism and the Sacred*, 4–8.

13   Rosemary Radford Ruether is the Carpenter Emerita Professor of Feminist Theology at Pacific School of Religion and the Graduate Theological Union in Berkeley, California, and Georgia Harkness Emerita Professor of Applied Theology at Garrett Evangelical Theological Seminary, Northwestern University, in Evanston, Illinois. She is one of the most prolific and significant contributors to religious and theological feminism in both North America and, arguably, the world.

14 Adams, *Ecofeminism and the Sacred*, 2; Steven Bouma-Prediger, *The Greening of Theology: The Ecological Models of Rosemary Radford Ruether, Joseph Sittler, and Jürgen Moltmann* (Atlanta: Scholars Press, 1995). According to Bouma-Prediger, Ruether was one of the first theologians to link liberation theology and a theology of nature and has consistently done so since the late 1960s. See Bouma-Prediger, *The Greening of Theology*, 12–14. See also Dieter T. Hessel, ed., *Theology for Earth Community: A Field Guide* (Maryknoll, NY: Orbis Books, 1996), 5–7.

15 Rosemary Radford Ruether, *New Woman/New Earth: Sexist Ideologies and Human Liberation* (New York: Seabury: 1975), 186. Elsewhere Ruether pithily writes: "We cannot criticize the hierarchy of male over female without ultimately criticizing and overcoming the hierarchy of human over nature" (*Sexism and God-Talk: Toward a Feminist Theology* [Boston: Beacon, 1983], 73).

16 Rosemary Radford Ruether, *Disputed Questions: On Being a Christian* (Maryknoll, NY: Orbis Books, 1989), 2.

17 Ruether, *Disputed Questions*, 2–3.

18 Ruether, *New Woman/New Earth*.

19 Rosemary Radford Ruether, "Rosemary Radford Ruether: Retrospective," *Religious Studies Review* 15 (January 1989); *Gaia & God: Toward an Ecofeminist Theology of Earth Healing* (San Francisco: HarperCollins, 1992), 205–53.

20 Ruether, "Rosemary Radford Ruether: Retrospective," 3.

21 Ruether, "Rosemary Radford Ruether: Retrospective," 3. Ruether critiques Lynn White's collapse of Hebraic and Christian views in "The Historical Roots of Our Ecologic Crisis" (see Ruether, *New Woman/New Earth*, 187).

22 This idea is also expressed in secular terms by Bill McKibben, who claims that "pristine" nature, unsmudged by humanity, is now gone, as traces of pollution are found even in polar regions. See Bill McKibben, *The End of Nature* (New York: Random House, 1989). It must be acknowledged, however, that grains, flowers, trees, and many types of animals have been cultivated and bred for centuries, representing a distinctive interaction between "nature" and humans.

23 Rosemary Radford Ruether, "Toward an Ecological–Feminist View of Nature," in *Healing the Wounds: The Promise of Ecofeminism*, ed. Judith Plant (Philadelphia: New Society, 1989), 149.

24 Ruether "Toward an Ecological–Feminist View of Nature," 149–50. Ruether's notion of "making friends" with the earth closely resembles the work of Passionist cultural historian Thomas Berry. See especially his book *Befriending the Earth: A Theology of Reconciliation between Humans and the Earth* (Mystic, CT: Twenty-Third Publications, 1991). (Thomas Berry takes pains to point out that the title actually originated with environmental philosopher Albert LaChance of the University of New Hampshire.) Such a construction of a new order is consistent with Ruether's understanding of the prophetic, liberative tradition. As she claims: "Liberation theology today consists not only in a discovery of this prophetic, transformative side of the tradition but also its recontextualization or restatement for today. Speaking a prophetic word of God is not simply an exegesis of past texts but the midrashic retelling of the story of liberation in the contemporary context. The Holy Spirit is a present, not simply a past, revelatory

power. Thus liberation theologies are not simply confined to what they can 'find' in past tradition. They are empowered to restate the vision in new dimensions, not imagined or only hinted at and undeveloped in the past" (Ruether, "Rosemary Radford Ruether: Retrospective," 3).

25   Ruether, *Gaia & God*, 4.

26   Ruether, *Gaia & God*, 57.

27   Ruether, *Gaia & God*, 265–72.

28   Ruether, *New Woman/New Earth*, 210.

29   Ruether, *New Woman/New Earth*, 211.

30   This colloquy, which has also nurtured intra–Third World dialogue, is manifest most tangibly in Rosemary Radford Ruether, ed., *Women Healing Earth: Third World Women on Ecology, Feminism, and Religion* (Maryknoll, NY: Orbis Books, 1996). Edited in collaboration with the ecofeminist Con-spirando Collective in Santiago, Chile, the volume includes contributions from Asia, Africa, and Latin America, including an article by Vandana Shiva, whose work is considered later in this chapter.

31   Ruether, *Women Healing Earth*, 5.

32   Sallie McFague is Distinguished Theologian in Residence at the Vancouver School of Theology in Vancouver, British Columbia, and professor emerita at Vanderbilt University in Nashville, Tennessee, where she taught for 30 years. She served as dean of the Vanderbilt Divinity School from 1975 to 1979 and has taught at Smith College, Yale Divinity School, and Harvard Divinity School.

33   Sallie McFague, "An Earthly Theological Agenda," in *Ecofeminism and the Sacred*, ed. Carol J. Adams (New York: Continuum, 1995), 86–87.

34   Sallie McFague, *Models of God: Theology for an Ecological, Nuclear Age* (Philadelphia: Fortress, 1987).

35   Sallie McFague, "Imaging a Theology of Nature: The World as God's Body," in *Liberating Life: Contemporary Approaches to Ecological Theology*, ed. Charles Birch, William Eakin, and Jay B. McDaniel (Maryknoll, NY: Orbis Books, 1990), 210.

36   Sallie McFague, *Models of God*; "Imaging a Theology of Nature," 211; "An Earthly Theological Agenda," 91.

37   McFague further clarifies her theological agenda: "I propose that one theological task is an experimental one with metaphors and models for the relationship between God and the world that will help bring about a theocentric, life-centered, cosmocentric sensibility in place of our anthropocentric one" ("Imaging a Theology of Nature," 202–03).

38   For a very accessible discussion of these models, see the interview with Sallie McFague in the video hosted by Bill Moyers entitled *Spirit and Nature*, based on a 1990 symposium at Middlebury College in Middlebury, Vermont.

39   McFague, "Imaging a Theology of Nature," 207.

40   McFague, "Imaging a Theology of Nature."

41   See Charles Hartshorne, "The Theological Analogies and the Cosmic Organism," in *Man's Vision of God and the Logic of Theism* (New York: Willett, Clark, and Co., 1941).

42 See the November 2003 article "Justice, Peace, and the Integrity of Creation," by D. Preman Niles, which gives the background information to the term, which was proposed by the World Council of Churches: http://www.wcc-coe.org/wcc/who/dictionary-article11.html (accessed May 14, 2012).

43 Sallie McFague, *The Body of God: An Ecological Theology* (Minneapolis: Fortress, 1993), 220.

44 McFague, *The Body of God*, 131–50.

45 McFague, *The Body of God*, 4. A Greenpeace television commercial graphically illustrates the future scenario McFague describes. In the ad, well-dressed businesspeople are walking, briefcases in hand, and all are wearing gas masks to screen out the brown, toxified air that surrounds them. A street person, *sans* gas mask, begs for and receives a token, which he then inserts into a public oxygen machine for some respiratory relief. The message is clear: in the future only the wealthy will be able to afford clean air. This trend is presently seen in the purchase of bottled water—many wealthy people, distrustful of the public water supply, increasingly procure water filters and bottled water, something that poor people cannot afford. This message, too, is becoming clear in North America (as it has been in the Third World for some time): only the affluent can afford safe drinking water.

46 McFague, *The Body of God*, 166.

47 McFague, *The Body of God*, 166. Brazilian liberation theologian Leonardo Boff also attempts to link oppression of the earth with oppression of poor persons, particularly indigenous peoples. See his *Ecology and Liberation: A New Paradigm* (Maryknoll, NY: Orbis Books, 1995). Influenced by contemporary science and process thought, McFague strives to show a compatibility between scientific theories of evolution and Christian solidarity with the poor. Contending that evolution is not entirely biological but also cultural and historical, McFague invokes Jesus' call to choose to be on the side of the oppressed and marginalized. We can now see that cultural evolution is of greater importance than natural selection, and we can have some say in the way we wish our culture to evolve on this planet. Cultural evolution is thus consistent with biological evolution in that both assert that there is a next phase of evolution, one that involves a sharing of the resources of the planet. It contradicts evolutionary science, however (and here McFague helpfully parts company with process theology), in that the principle for this new evolutionary step to occur relies not on natural selection but on human solidarity with all, especially the outcasts and oppressed (*The Body of God*, 171–74).

48 McFague, *The Body of God*, 109.

49 McFague, "Imaging a Theology of Nature," 216–17. For an examination of the ecological implications of this notion of "household," see Stephen B. Scharper and Hilary Cunningham, *The Green Bible* (New York: Lantern Books, 2001).

50 McFague, *The Body of God*, 178.

51 Vandana Shiva is founder of the Research Foundation of Science, Technology, and Natural Resource Policy near Delhi. After receiving a doctorate in theoretical physics, she worked for the Indian Institute for Management in Bangalore and continues to devote time to the Chipko movement, a women's "tree-hugger" initiative in India. As Rosemary Radford Ruether writes, "The person who has taken the lead in shaping ...

social feminism, for Indians in particular and for Asian women generally, is Vandana Shiva" (Ruether, *Women Healing Earth*, 61).

52 Vandana Shiva, "Let Us Survive: Women, Ecology, and Development," in Ruether, *Women Healing Earth*, 73.

53 For a fine case study of SAPs and their effect on Third World ecology, agriculture, and people, see John Mihevc, *The Market Tells Them So: The World Bank and Economic Fundamentalism in Africa* (Penang, Malaysia: Third World Network, 1995). What Shiva describes as the "monoculture" of such developmentalist programs Mihevc describes as a "fundamentalist theology," especially in terms of the World Bank.

54 Vandana Shiva, *Monocultures of the Mind: Perspectives on Biodiversity and Biotechnology* (London: Zed Books, 1993), 7.

55 Shiva, *Monocultures of the Mind*, 1–45.

56 Shiva, "Let Us Survive," 66.

57 Vandana Shiva, *Staying Alive: Women, Ecology, and Development* (London: Zed Books, 1989), 1–13; "Let Us Survive," 65–67.

58 Shiva, *Staying Alive*, 80–85.

59 An example of such "maldevelopment," according to Shiva, is the Mahaweli Development Program in Sri Lanka. Adopting a short-term vantage, the project built dams across Sri Lanka's longest river, which led to deforestation and an altered landscape, as well as the displacement of thousands of peasant families, who were then resettled. In addition to ecological destruction, the project led to social unrest, for the resettlement resulted in a majority Sinhalese community in the Eastern Province of Sri Lanka, an area that had a heretofore balanced ethnic composition ("Let Us Survive," 72).

60 Shiva, *Staying Alive*, 82.

61 Shiva, *Staying Alive*, 82.

62 Vandana Shiva, *Ecology and the Politics of Survival: Conflicts over Natural Resources in India* (Tokyo: United Nations University Press, 1991), 346.

63 Shiva "Let Us Survive," 67–70. Shiva further elucidates this connection between science and sexism: "Modern science was a consciously gendered patriarchal activity. As nature came to be seen more like a woman to be raped, gender too was recreated. Science as a male venture, based on the subjugation of female nature and female sex, provided support for the polarization of gender. Patriarchy as the new scientific and technological power was a political need of emerging industrial capitalism. While, on the one hand, the ideology of science sanctioned the denudation of nature, on the other, it legitimized the dependency of women and the authority of men. Science and masculinity were associated in domination over nature and all that is seen as feminine" ("Let Us Survive," 69).

64 Shiva, *Monocultures of the Mind*.

65 Shiva, *Monocultures of the Mind*, 60.

66 Vandana Shiva, *The Violence of the Green Revolution: Third World Agriculture, Ecology, and Politics* (London: Zed Books, 1991).

67 Shiva, *Monocultures of the Mind*, 1–45.

68   Shiva, *Monocultures of the Mind*, 96–131.

69   See J. R. Kloppenburg, *First the Seed: The Political Economy of Plant Biotechnology* (Cambridge: Cambridge University Press, 1988).

70   Shiva, *Monocultures of the Mind*, 112.

71   Shiva, *Monocultures of the Mind*, 110–13.

72   Shiva, *Monocultures of the Mind*, 145.

73   Shiva, "Let Us Survive," 70–71. Women's ecological movements are not simply found in the Third World. In North America, for example, Roman Catholic women religious are becoming deeply involved in ecological ministry. Many congregations are devoting money and members to ecological projects. Among the most prominent of these are Sr. Miriam Therese McGillis and Sr. Paula Gonzalez, both of whom help coordinate sustainable, ecologically sensitive communities. Others include Sr. Janis Yeakel, ASC, of Earthworks in Plymouth, Indiana, and Sr. Virginia Jones of the Nazareth Center for Ecological Spirituality in Kalamazoo, Michigan. Just as women religious were the first to take the teachings of Vatican II seriously, allowing the conciliar documents to permeate their chapters and help restructure their organizations, so too are they taking the lead in the Catholic religious environmental movement. In addition to establishing full- and part-time "eco-ministries," many orders have had environmental audits done of their properties, leading to energy-saving measures, recycling, organic farming, and the creation of wildlife sanctuaries.

74   Shiva, *Monocultures of the Mind*, 20ff. The Chipko movement's inaugural action occurred in March 1973 in Gopeshwar village, where thirty ash trees in the region had been granted to a sporting goods producer by forest authorities. Gaura Devi, a widow in her fifties, with most of the men out of town collecting land compensation, allegedly stood before a gun-wielding tree "harvester," claiming that the forest is her people's *maika* (mother's home) and saying that if the trees were taken, landslides would devastate their fields and homes. She and her companions forced the enraged loggers to leave without their timber. See Pamela Philipose, "Women Act: Women and Environmental Protection in India," in *Healing the Wounds: The Promise of Ecofeminism*, ed. Judith Plant (Philadelphia: New Society, 1989).

75   Shiva, *Staying Alive*.

76   Shiva, *Monocultures of the Mind*, 133ff.

77   Shiva, *Monocultures of the Mind*, 88–93.

78   A starting point for this polyvalent relationship with nature is perhaps taking a look at concrete historical examples of women's ecological activity. Shiva does this admirably with the Chipko movement. Ruether and McFague, in contrast, along with some other ecofeminists, tend to be less concrete in their analysis, avoiding or neglecting such critical North American environmental advocates as author Susan Fenimore Cooper, artist Deborah Passmore, and biologist Rachel Carson (Vera Norwood, *Made from This Earth: American Women and Nature* [Chapel Hill, NC: University of North Carolina Press, 1993], 275–84; I am indebted to Max Oelschlaeger for suggesting this source). Moreover, as suggested, the transformative work presently being done by Roman Catholic sisters to promote ecological sustainability goes apparently unmentioned in their analysis.

From Community to Communion: The Natural City in Biotic and Cosmological Perspective

1   Raymond Williams, *The Country and the City* (New York: Oxford University Press, 1985).

2   Williams, *The Country and the City*, 1.

3   Ebenezer Howard, *Garden Cities of To-morrow* (London: Faber and Faber, 1898), 42.

4   Stephen M. Wheeler and Timothy Beatley, eds., *The Sustainable Urban Development Reader* (London: Routledge, 2004), 279.

5   Lewis Mumford, *The Culture of Cities* (New York: Harcourt, 1938), 139.

6   Wheeler and Beatley, *The Sustainable Urban Development Reader*, 7.

7   Mumford, *The Culture of Cities*, 142.

8   Ian L. McHarg, *Design with Nature* (Wilmington, DE: Wiley-Liss, 1969).

9   Wheeler and Beatley, *The Sustainable Urban Development Reader*, 35.

10 McHarg, *Design with Nature*, 58.

11 Wheeler and Beatley, *The Sustainable Urban Development Reader*, 113.

12 Anne Whiston Spirn, *The Granite Garden* (New York: Basic Books, 1984), 98.

13 This movement has been faulted, however, for insufficient attention to affordable housing; non-incorporation of green design, architecture, and landscape techniques; and selecting sites, such as Duany's Seaside, outside of pre-existing urban areas. (Wheeler and Beatley, *The Sustainable Urban Development Reader*, 74.)

14 Peter Calthorpe, *The Next American Metropolis: Ecology, Community and the American Dream* (Princeton, NJ: Princeton Architectural Press, 1993), 122.

15 Susan Flader, *Thinking Like a Mountain: Aldo Leopold and the Evolution of an Ecological Attitude Toward Deer, Wolves and Forests* (Columbia, MO: University of Missouri Press, 1974), 32.

16 Aldo Leopold, "Thinking Like a Mountain," in *A Sand County Almanac: And Sketches Here and There* (New York: Oxford University Press, 1948), 129.

17 Leopold, "Thinking Like a Mountain," 132.

18 Leopold, "Thinking Like a Mountain," 135.

19 Leopold, "Thinking Like a Mountain," 203.

20 Thomas Berry, *Befriending the Earth: Toward a Theology of Reconciliation Between Humans and the Earth* (Mystic, CT: 1991), 51.

21 Berry, *Befriending the Earth*, 73.

22 Berry, *Befriending the Earth*, 35.

23 Berry, *The Dream of the Earth* (San Francisco: Sierra Club Books, 1988), 48–49.

24 Lerner, *The Politics of Meaning*, 59.

25 Berry, *Befriending the Earth*, 132.

26 While Spirn seems closest among the urban voices surveyed to Leopold's notion of a biotic community, she still uses the modern language of mastery in relationship to the

natural ecosystem, noting that cities "have mostly neglected and rarely exploited the natural forces within them," and that the "social value of nature must be recognized and its power harnessed, rather than resisted. Nature in a city," she argues, "must be cultivated, like a garden, rather than ignored or subdued" (Spirn, *The Granite Garden*, 87). Although signalling a major advance over ecologically pernicious urban attitudes, Spirn nevertheless seems to view the human as land manager—a benevolent cultivating gardener, to be sure, but one who still "exploits" and "harnesses" nature for his or her own benefit. (I am speaking here strictly here of Spirn's 1984 text, and not her later writings.) This is a different understanding than Leopold's view of the human as "just plain citizen" within the biotic community, and an even further cry from Henry David Thoreau's insight that "in wildness is the preservation of the world."

Option for the Poor and Option for the Earth: Toward a Sustainable Solidarity

1   I wish to thank Gustavo Gutiérrez and Daniel Groody for suggesting this article but also for the cogent commitments to a more just and life-giving world that underlie it.

2   For a gripping account of the Bhopal tragedy, see *Five Past Midnight in Bhopal* by Dominique Lapierre and Javier Moro, trans. Kathryn Spink (London: Scribner, 2002). See also Martin Regg Cohn, "Death Stalks Bhopal 20 Years Later: 15,300 Killed in Wake of Disaster" (*The Toronto Star*, November 27, 2004), pp. 1, 22; and Lindalee Tracey, Peter Raymount, and Harold Crooks, prod. and dir., *Bhopal: The Search for Justice* (November 2004), Toronto: National Film Board of Canada.

3   Lapierre and Moro, *Five Past Midnight in Bhopal*, 202–03.

4   Donal Dorr, *Option for the Poor: A Hundred Years of Catholic Social Teaching* (Maryknoll, NY: Orbis Books, [revised ed.], 1992), 4. Dorr further describes the import of such solidarity, which implies "commitment to working and living within structures and agencies that promote the interests of the less favored sectors of society. These would include those who are economically poor, the groups that are politically marginalized or oppressed, people discriminated against on sexual grounds, peoples that have been culturally silenced or oppressed, and those who have been religiously disinherited or deprived." Dorr, *Option for the Poor*.

5   Gustavo Gutiérrez, "Option for the Poor: Assessment and Implications," *ARC: The Journal of the Faculty of Religious Studies, McGill University* (1994), 66.

6   "The Meaning and Scope of Medellin," in Gustavo Gutiérrez, *The Density of the Present: Selected Writings* (Maryknoll, NY: Orbis Books, 1999), 98.

7   Gutiérrez, *The Density of the Present*, 98.

8   Gutiérrez, *The Density of the Present*, 98.

9   Gutiérrez, *The Density of the Present*, 98.

10   Gutiérrez, *The Density of the Present*, 67. In a related fashion, according to Harvard biologist E. O. Wilson, humans are forcing into extinction daily hundreds of species of flora and fauna that have never been identified or classified. In this sense, both the nameless perishing poor and the undesignated dying species share a grim solidarity of anonymous deaths.

11   Gustavo Gutiérrez, *A Theology of Liberation* (Maryknoll, NY: Orbis Books, 1973), 36–37.

12   Gutiérrez, "Contestation in Latin America," in *Contestation in the Church*, ed. T. Jimenez (New York: Herder and Herder, 1971), 43.

13   Walt W. Rostow, *The Stages of Economic Growth: A Non-Communist Manifesto* (London and New York: Oxford University Press, 1962).

14   Alex Inkeles, "The Modernization of Man," in Myron Weiner, ed. *Modernization: The Dynamics of Growth* (New York: Basic Books, 1966), 138–50.

15   David C. McClelland, "The Impulse to Modernize," in Weiner, ed. *Modernization*, 34–35.

16   Talcott Parsons, *Societies: Evolutionary and Comparative Perspectives* (Englewood Cliffs, NJ: Prentice-Hall, 1966).

17   June Nash, "Ethnographic Aspects of the World Capitalist System," *Annual Review of Anthropology*, Vol. 10 (1981):407.

18   See Andre Gunder Frank, *Capitalism and Underdevelopment in Latin America* (New York: Monthly Review Press, 1967) and *Latin America: Underdevelopment or Revolution?* (New York: Monthly Review Press, 1969).

19   Immanuel Wallerstein, *The Modern World System* (New York: Academic, 1975).

20   Gutiérrez, *A Theology of Liberation*, 36.

21   Gutiérrez, "Faith as Freedom: Solidarity with the Alienated and Confidence in the Future," *Horizons* 2:1 (Spring 1995):30–31.

22   Enrique Dussel, *The Underside of Modernity: Apel, Ricoeur, Rorty, Taylor and the Philosophy of Liberation*, trans. and ed. Eduardo Mendieta (Atlantic Highlands, NJ: Humanities Press, 1996), 2–3. For further critiques of globalization from a liberationist vantage, see Jon Sobrino and Felix Wilfed, eds., *Globalization and Its Victims*, Concilium 5 (2001) (London: SCM Press).

23   Gustavo Gutiérrez, *The Truth Shall Make You Free: Confrontations* (Maryknoll, NY: Orbis Books, 1990), 136–37.

24   For a perturbing account of the destruction of the Amazon rainforest of Brazil and its aboriginal occupants, see Adrian Cowell, dir. and prod., *Decade of Destruction* (Oley, PA: Bullfrog Films, 1990, 270 min.).

25   The World Commission on Environment and Development, *Our Common Future* (New York: Oxford University Press, 1987), 43. I am indebted to Ingrid Leman Stefanovic for her fertile critique of sustainable development from a phenomenological perspective.

26   The World Commission on Environment and Development, *Our Common Future*, 39.

27   The notion of sustainable development has also been critiqued for its basis in "calculative," positivistic thinking rather than more "originative," holistic mode of inquiry, leading to a less-than-substantive rethinking of the human–earth relationship called for in our present ecological moment. See Ingrid Leman Stefanovic, "Evolving Sustainability: A Rethinking of Ontological Foundations," *Trumpeter Journal of Ecosophy* 8:4 (Fall 1991):194–200. See also Stefanovic, *Safeguarding Our Common Future: Rethinking Sustainable Development* (Albany: State University of New York Press, 2000).

28 The Episcopal Commission for Social Affairs, Canadian Conference of Catholic Bishops, "Ethical Reflections on the Economic Crisis," December 22, 1982. (Reprinted in *Do Justice! The Social Teaching of the Canadian Catholic Bishops*, ed. E. F. Sheridan, S.J., Sherbrooke, QC, and Toronto: Éditions Paulines and the Jesuit Centre for Social Faith and Justice, 1987, par. 15, p. 417.)

29 The Episcopal Commission for Social Affairs, Canadian Conference of Catholic Bishops, "Ethical Reflections on the Economic Crisis," in Sheridan, *Do Justice!*, par. 17, p. 418.

30 Ramachandra Guha, "Radical American Environmentalism and Wilderness Preservation: A Third World Critique, *Environmental Ethics* 11 (1):296–305.

31 Leonardo Boff, *Ecology and Liberation: A New Paradigm* (Maryknoll, NY: Orbis Books, 1995), 102.

32 Dussel, *The Underside of Modernity*, 20.

33 These points are more fully developed in Dussel's *The Invention of the Americas: Eclipse of the "Other" and the Myth of Modernity* (New York: Continuum, 1995).

34 Dussel, *The Underside of Modernity*, 21.

35 For a fuller discussion of Boff and Gebara, see my *Redeeming the Time* (New York: Continuum, 1987), 165–83.

36 For an overview of some of these groups, see Marie Price, "Ecopolitics and Environmental Nongovernmental Organizations in Latin America," *The Geographical Review* 84:1 (January, 1994):42–58.

37 Lee Cormie, "Movements of the Spirit in History," in Mario DeGiglio-Bellemare and Gabriella Mirand Garcia *Talitha cum! The Grace of Solidarity in a Globalized World*, ed. (Geneva: World Student Christian Federation Publications, 2004), 238–60, 249–50. See also the World Social Forum web page: http://www.forumsocialmundial.org.br and http://www.choike.org/nuevo_eng/informes/1557.html. The author wishes to thank Lee Cormie for suggesting these resources.

38 See Sarah McFarland Taylor, "Reinhabiting Religion: Green Sisters, Ecological Renewal, and the Biography of Religious Landscape." *Worldviews* 6:3 (2002): 227–52. For a lively integration of Thomas Berry and Brian Swimme's work within a social justice framework, see the work of Jim Conlon, especially *At the Edge of Our Longing* (Ottawa, ON: Novalis, 2004).

39 You can get a good idea of the meaning and impact of ecological debt by reading the following passage written by Aurora Donoso, of Acción Ecológica, Amigos de la Tierra in Ecuador, entitled "Ecological Debt: The Desecration of Life." It can be found at http://www.ecologicaldebt.org/Resource-Extraction-Debt/Ecological-debt-the-desecration-of-life.html:

When ancestral knowledge and seeds have been appropriated and utilized.

When science is used to produce hybrid or genetically modified seeds, breaking reproductive cycles for the benefit of transnational corporations which patent life, and attack the food sovereignty of the peoples.

When monocultures are promoted and agro toxics are made in order to alter life's natural cycles, degrading the land, the water and the air, and affecting the health of the campesinos.

When natural goods are extracted in order to feed industry, at the cost of the social and environmental destruction of the countries of the Third World and the planet in general, and an environmentally unequal trade is established.

When even the planet's atmosphere and carbon sinks are appropriated without assuming any commitment or responsibility for their destruction, and for the effects of climate change.

When toxic waste is produced and deposited in Third World countries, especially in the poorest areas.

When the illegitimate, inhuman, and immoral, external debt, which has already been paid, is used to enslave people to the service of capital and to sustaining this flow of natural goods, cheap labour, and financial resources from South to North.

When chemical, biological and nuclear weapons are produced, tested and sold to our countries, and when they make loans to buy these weapons.

When due to this flow of cheap resources over production is encouraged, and as a consequence over consumption and over generation of waste, which are destroying our sources of livelihood and the life of the planet. All of which they now intend to sell us as "Free Trade".

When the desecration of life has reached such a point that the industrialized countries have even stolen the genes of the most isolated indigenous communities for the human genome project.

And now they dare to publicly state that they have deciphered the language of God!

All these forms of appropriation, destruction, and alteration of life, carried out principally by the industrialized countries of the North, are what we call the ecological debt, which those countries owe to the countries of the Third World and the planet.

40   See the Canadian Ecumenical Jubilee Initiative (CEJI), *Sacred Earth, Sacred Community: Jubilee, Ecology, and Aboriginal Peoples* (Toronto: CEJI, 2000).

41   I am indebted to Hilary Cunningham for suggesting this term.

Conclusion: From Sustainable Development to Sustainable Liberation: Toward an Anthropo-harmonic Ethic

1   See Stephen Scharper, "Democracy, Cosmology, and *The Great Work*," *Worldviews: Environment, Culture and Religion* 5, nos. 2 and 3 (2001): 190 or http://www.thomasberry.org/Essays/DemocracyCosmologyAndTheGreatWorkOfThomasBerry.html (accessed May 14, 2012).

Sources

Articles and other publications in this volume are reprinted with permission. Below is a list of where they originally appeared.

Section I: Revealing—The Pain of Loss and the Delight in Wonder

"Reverend Billy's Crusade against the 'Shopocalypse,'" *The Toronto Star*, December 22, 2007.

"The Rise of Nature Deficit Disorder," *The Toronto Star*, August 11, 2007.

"Green Dreams: Religious Cosmologies and Environmental Commitments," *Bulletin of Science, Technology, and Society*, Volume 22 (1) (February 2002): 42–45.

"Poor Bear Burden of Environmental Hazards," *The Toronto Star*, November 25, 2006.

"Truth, Lies, and Broadcasting in Canada," *The Toronto Star*, January 24, 2011.

"The Ecological Crisis." *The Twentieth Century: A Theological Perspective*, edited by Gregory Baum, Ottawa, ON/ Maryknoll, NY: Novalis/ Orbis Books, 1999, 219–27.

Section II: Reflecting—What on Earth Are We Doing?

"We All Lose in the War Against Nature," *The Toronto Star*, April 16, 2010.

"O Ye of Little Eco-Faith," *The Toronto Star*, April 28, 2007.

"The Gaia Theory: Implications for a Christian Political Theology of the Environment," *Cross Currents*, Volume 44 (2) (Summer 1994): 207–21. (Originally entitled "The Gaia Hypothesis," but changed to reflect its current status.)

"Born Again: Liberation Theology," *The Toronto Star*, December 1, 2007.

"Ecofeminism: From Patriarchy to Mutuality." Chapter 5 of *Redeeming the Time: A Political Theology of the Environment*, New York: Continuum Publishing Company, 1998 (paper), 132–83.

"The Gulf of Mexico Oil Spill," Interview by Paul Fraumeni, University of Toronto "Research and Innovation" website, May 28, 2010.

Section III: Redeeming—A Creative Space for New Life-giving Relationships

"From Corpse to Compost," *The Toronto Star*, June 10, 2006.

"The Bride Wore … Green," *The Toronto Star*, April 26, 2008.

"From Community to Communion: The Natural City in Biotic and Cosmological Perspective." In *The Natural City: Re-envisioning the Built Environment*, co-edited with Ingrid Stefanovic, Toronto: University of Toronto Press, 2012, 89–103.

"The Ethics of Organic Farming," *The Toronto Star*, January 22, 2010.

"Option for the Poor and Option for the Earth: Toward a Sustainable Solidarity." In *Option for the Poor: An Interdisciplinary Perspective*, edited by Gustavo Gutiérrez and Daniel Groody. Forthcoming from University of Notre Dame Press.

"On Sacrifice, Spirituality, and Silver Linings," *The Toronto Star*, December 29, 2002.

"Christmas Invites Us to Make Peace on Earth a Reality," *The Toronto Star*, December 24, 2010.

Appendix
Suggested Readings and Viewings

The following books and documentaries are presented here to help you participate more deeply with Scharper's analysis and reflections. He refers to many of these works in his writings. They are divided here into categories for ease of reference, according to their main area of concern. However, our categorization does not limit their scope, as many of these works touch upon many subjects and issues that could place them easily in other categories.

On the Universe Story

Berry, Thomas. *The Dream of the Earth*. San Francisco: Sierra Club Books, 1988.

Cosmic Voyage. A documentary with Morgan Freeman as narrator. It projects the grandeur and big picture of our vast Universe as never seen before. National Air and Space Museum, 1996. 36 min.

Journey of the Universe: The Epic Story of Cosmic, Earth, and Human Transformation. A documentary on the story of the universe and its potential to change our civilization, created by Brian Swimme and Mary Evelyn Tucker. Northcutt Productions, 2011. 56 min.

Swimme, Brian. *The Hidden Heart of the Cosmos: Humanity and the New Story*. Maryknoll, NY: Orbis Books, 1996.

Swimme, Brian, and Thomas Berry. *The Universe Story: From the Primordial Flaring Forth to the Ecozoic Era: A Celebration of the Unfolding of the Cosmos*. San Francisco: HarperCollins, 1992.

Swimme, Brian, and Mary Evelyn Tucker. *Journey of the Universe*. New Haven, CT: Yale University Press, 2011. (This book is a good accompaniment to the documentary above of the same name.)

On Liberation and Ecology

Boff, Leonardo. *Cry of the Earth, Cry of the Poor*. Translated by Philip Berryman. Maryknoll, NY: Orbis Books, 1997.

Boff, Leonardo. *Ecology and Liberation: A New Paradigm*. Maryknoll, NY: Orbis Books, 1995.

Conway, Janet M. *Edges of Global Justice: The World Social Forum and Its "Others."* New York: Routledge, 2012.

Dorr, Donal. *Option for the Poor: A Hundred Years of Catholic Social Teaching*. Maryknoll, NY: Orbis Books, 1992.

Dussel, Enrique. *The Invention of the Americas: Eclipse of the "Other" and the Myth of Modernity*. New York: Continuum, 1995.

Dussel, Enrique. *The Underside of Modernity: Apel, Ricoeur, Rorty, Taylor and the Philosophy of Liberation*. Translated and edited by Eduardo Mendieta. Atlantic Highlands, NJ: Humanities Press, 1996.

Gutiérrez. Gustavo. *A Theology of Liberation: History, Politics, and Salvation*, 15th anniversary edition. Maryknoll, NY: Orbis Books, 1988.

Gutiérrez, Gustavo. *The Truth Shall Make You Free: Confrontations*. Maryknoll, NY: Orbis Books, 1990.

Petrella, Ivan. *The Future of Liberation Theology: An Argument and Manifesto*. London: SCM Press, 2006.

Wisdoms from the Natural and Social Sciences

Capra, Fritjof. *The Turning Point: Science, Society, and the Rising Culture*. New York: Simon and Schuster, 1982.

Carson, Rachel. *Silent Spring*. 40th anniversary edition. Boston: Houghton Mifflin, 2002.

Cobb, John B., Jr. *Sustainability: Economics, Ecology and Justice*. Maryknoll, NY: Orbis Books, 1992.

Frank, Andre Gunder. *Capitalism and Underdevelopment in Latin America*. New York: Monthly Review Press, 1967.

Hathaway, Mark, and Leonardo Boff. *The Tao of Liberation: Exploring the Ecology of Transformation*. Maryknoll, NY: Orbis Books, 2009.

Hawken, Paul. *The Ecology of Commerce: A Declaration of Sustainability*. New York: HarperCollins, 1993.

Korten, David C. *Agenda for a New Economy: From Phantom Wealth to Real Wealth*. San Francisco: Berrett-Koehler Publishers, 2009.

Lovelock, James E. *Gaia: A New Look at Life on Earth*. New York: Oxford University Press, 1995.

Margulis, Lynn. *Symbiotic Planet: A New Look at Evolution*. New York: Basic Books, 1998.

Shiva, Vandana. *Monocultures of the Mind: Perspectives on Biodiversity and Biotechnology*. London: Zed Books, 1993.

Westra, Laura, and Peter S. Wentz. *Faces of Environmental Racism: Confronting Issues of Global Justice*. Lanham, MD: Rowan and Littlefield, 1995.

On Ecofeminism

Eaton, Heather. *Introducing Ecofeminist Theologies*. New York: T&T Clark International, 2005.

McFague, Sallie. *The Body of God: An Ecological Theology*. Minneapolis: Fortress Press, 1993.

McFague, Sallie. *Models of God: Theology for an Ecological, Nuclear Age*. Philadelphia: Fortress Press, 1987.

Ruether, Rosemary Radford. *Gaia & God: An Ecofeminist Theology of Earth Healing*. San Francisco: HarperCollins, 1992.

Ruether, Rosemary Radford. *New Woman/New Earth: Sexist Ideologies and Human Liberation.* New York: Seabury, 1975.

Ruether, Rosemary Radford. *Women Healing Earth: Third World Women on Ecology, Feminism, and Religion.* Maryknoll, NY: Orbis Books, 1996.

Shiva, Vandana, and Maria Miles. *Ecofeminism.* London: Zed Books, 1993.

Aboriginal Wisdom

Deloria, Vine, Jr. *God Is Red: A Native View of Religion.* Golden, CO: Fulcrum Publications, 2003.

Grim, John A., editor. *Indigenous Traditions and Ecology: The Interbeing of Cosmology and Community.* Cambridge, MA: Harvard University Press for the Center for the Study of World Religions, Harvard Divinity School, 2001.

The Iroquois Speak Out for Mother Earth. A documentary featuring interviews with Iroquois elders and their view on our relationship with Earth. The Artist's/Environment Forum, directed and produced by Danny Beaton, a Mohawk of the Turtle Clan, Toronto, 2009. 51 min.

Leduc, Timothy B. *Climate, Culture, Change: Inuit and Western Dialogues with a Warming North.* Ottawa: University of Ottawa Press, 2010.

More on "What on Earth Are We Doing?"

The Corporation. A documentary that looks at the concept of the corporation throughout recent history up to its present-day dominance. Big Picture Media Corporation, 2003. 145 min.

The Cove. A documentary portraying the work of a group of activists, led by renowned dolphin trainer Ric O'Barry, who infiltrates a cove near Taijii, Japan, to expose both a shocking instance of animal abuse and a serious threat to human health. Diamond Docs, Fish Films, and Oceanic Preservation Society. 2009. 92 min.

Food, Inc. A documentary that takes an unflattering look inside America's corporate-controlled food industry. Magnolia Pictures, Participant Media, and River Road Entertainment, 2008. 94 min.

An Inconvenient Truth. A documentary on Al Gore's campaign to make the issue of global warming a recognized problem worldwide. Lawrence Bender Productions and Participant Productions, 2006. 100 min.

Kozol, Jonathan. *Amazing Grace: The Lives of Children and the Conscience of a Nation.* New York: Crown, 1995.

Louv, Richard. *Last Child in the Woods: Saving Our Children from Nature-deficit Disorder.* Chapel Hill, NC: Algonquin Books of Chapel Hill, 2008.

Louv, Richard. *The Nature Principle.* Chapel Hill, NC: Algonquin Books, 2012.

Lovelock, James E. *The Revenge of Gaia: Why the Earth Is Fighting Back and How We Can Still Save Humanity.* London: Penguin Books, 2007.

Manufactured Landscapes. Photographer Edward Burtynsky travels the world observing changes in landscapes due to industrial work and manufacturing. Foundry Films and the National Film Board of Canada, 2006. 80 min.

McKibben, Bill. *The End of Nature*, with a new introduction by the author. New York: Random House, 2006.

Mitchell, Alanna. *Sea Sick: The Global Ocean in Crisis.* Toronto: McClelland & Stewart, 2009.

Nash, Knowlton. *Trivia Pursuit: How Showbiz Values Are Corrupting the News.* Toronto: McClelland & Stewart, 1998.

Orr, David W. *Earth in Mind: On Education, Environment, and the Human Prospect*, 10th anniversary edition. Washington, DC: Island Press, 2004.

What Would Jesus Buy? A documentary that examines the commercialization of Christmas in America while following Reverend Billy and the Church of Stop Shopping on a cross-country mission to save Christmas from the "Shopocalypse." The film delves into issues of sweatshops, debt, and consumerism. Palisades Pictures, Warrior Poet, and Werner films, 2007. 90 min.

Who Killed the Electric Car? A documentary with Martin Sheen as narrator. An investigation of the birth and death of the electric car, as well as the role of renewable energy and sustainable living in the future. Plinyminor, Electric Entertainment, and Papercut Films, 2006. 92 min. (See also the 2011 sequel, *The Revenge of the Electric Car.*)

On Reimagining the Role of the Human

Baraka. A documentary that journeys throughout the planet with expertly photographed scenes and without dialogue exploring our deep spiritual appreciation of our world. Magidson Films, 1992. 96 min.

Berry, Thomas. *The Sacred Universe: Earth, Spirituality, and Religion in the Twenty-first Century.* Edited and with a foreword by Mary Evelyn Tucker. New York: Columbia University Press, 2009.

Berry, Thomas, with Thomas Clarke, SJ. *Befriending the Earth.* Mystic, CT: Twenty-Third Publications, 1991.

Fierce Light: When Spirit Meets Action. A documentary capturing the exciting movement of spiritual activism that is exploding around the planet, and some of the powerful personalities who are igniting it. FierceLight Films, Big Picture Media Corporation, and National Film Board of Canada, 2008. 90 min.

Hawken, Paul. *Blessed Unrest: How the Largest Movement in the World Came into Being, and Why No One Saw It Coming.* New York: Viking, 2007.

Leopold, Aldo. *A Sand County Almanac: And Sketches Here and There.* New York: Oxford University Press, 1948.

The Sacred Balance. A four-part documentary series with David Suzuki that celebrates the meeting of science and spirit. Bullfrog Films, 2003. Each part, 54 min.

Scharper, Stephen Bede. *Redeeming the Time: A Political Theology of the Environment.* New York: Continuum, 1997.

Scharper, Stephen Bede, and Hilary Cunningham. *The Green Bible.* New York: Lantern, 2001.

Shiva, Vandana. *Earth Democracy: Justice, Sustainability, and Peace.* Cambridge, MA: South End Press, 2005.

Stefanovic, Ingrid Leman. *Safeguarding Our Common Future: Rethinking Sustainable Development.* Albany, NY: State University of New York Press, 2000.

Stefanovic, Ingrid Leman, and Stephen Bede Scharper, eds. *The Natural City: Re-envisioning the Built Environment.* Toronto: University of Toronto Press, 2012.

Suzuki, David, with Amanda McConnell and Adrienne Mason. *The Sacred Balance: Rediscovering Our Place in Nature*, updated and expanded version. Vancouver: Greystone Books, 2007. (This book is a good accompaniment to the documentary above of the same name.)

Taylor, Sarah McFarland. *Green Sisters: A Spiritual Ecology.* Cambridge, MA: Harvard University Press, 2007.